W9-BMX-743

VEGAN BITES

RECIPES FOR SINGLES

BEVERLY LYNN BENNETT

BOOK PUBLISHING COMPANY
Summertown, Tennessee

Library of Congress Cataloging-in-Publication Data

Bennett, Beverly Lynn.
    Vegan bites : recipes for singles / by Beverly Lynn Bennett.
        p.   cm.
    Includes index.
    ISBN 978-1-57067-221-7
    1. Vegan cookery 2. Cookery for one. 1. Title.

    TX837.B46275 2008
    641.5'636—dc22   007050628

Cover and interior design: *Aerocraft Charter Art Service*

Printed in Canada

Book Publishing Company
P.O. Box 99
Summertown, TN 38483
888-260-8458
www.bookpubco.com

ISBN 13: 978-1-57067-221-0

17 16 15 14 13 12 11 10 09 08 1 2 3 4 5 6 7 8 9

Book Publishing Co. is a member of
Green Press Initiative. We chose to print
this title on paper with postconsumer
recycled content, processed without
chlorine, which saved the following
natural resources:

62 trees

2,921 lbs of solid waste

22,751 gallons of water

5,481 lbs pounds of greenhouse gases

43 million BTUs of total energy

For more information, visit
www.greenpressinitiative.org.

*(Paper calculations from Environmental Defense
Paper Calculator www.papercalculator.org)*

BOOK
PUBLISHING
COMPANY

green
press
INITIATIVE

CONTENTS

Acknowledgments

There are several people that I would like to thank for their loving support and assistance during the writing of this book:

Cynthia and Bob Holzapfel, for their commitment in producing and publishing so many wonderful pro-vegan and vegetarian lifestyle books and cookbooks, and for inviting me to be a part of their respected family of authors.

Jo Stepaniak, my friend and editor on this project, for all of her insights, words of wisdom, patience, and guidance from the very beginning to the final completion of this book.

My husband, Ray Sammartano, for his constructive input as well as his brave and tireless taste testing during the recipe development process.

Luna, my feline companion, for the many purring sessions and snuggling lovefests on my lap while I sat at the computer working on this book.

And lastly, all the vegans in the world, for choosing to improve your lives, the lives of animals, and the future of this planet. Thank you for living consciously and making a difference.

GETTING STARTED

Young and Ambitious

The vegan community is made up of millions of concerned, passionate, and devoted people. They've all experienced one of the most profound epiphanies of the modern world: we share life on this planet with other animals, and we need to work together as friends and not fight, harm, hurt, or eat each other. It's so simple and yet so true.

With many of the growing global and environmental concerns being linked to animal agriculture, young, ambitious vegans are opting to follow in the footsteps of their parents and other concerned citizens whose activism grew out of the sixties and seventies. In an attempt to makes serious changes in the ways that people use and abuse animals, they're proactively voicing their concerns to governmental agencies and business and industry through writing letters, creating blogs and websites, staging protests, and participating in demonstrations.

Many young people naturally gravitate toward a more compassionate life. They love animals and consider them sweet, innocent friends. Seeing no real difference between the life of a cat and that of a cow, they logically decide they no longer want to eat their animal friends or use products that are the result of inhumane treatment. Increasing numbers of young people are making this choice a lifetime commitment, even going as far as skipping the common first step of becoming vegetarian and instead going totally vegan right from the start.

This book was written specifically for single young people (in their teens and twenties) who have chosen to live as vegans. It provides practical advice and guidance so you can fend for yourself and cook for one, whether you're still living at home and relying on your folks, sharing a place with roommates, or out on your own. In case anyone is concerned that you might become malnourished, I've included a short overview of how to fulfill your nutritional needs, from food sources to serving sizes.

All too often, single people find themselves at the mercy of restaurants and fast food. To avoid that pitfall and wisely budget your money, you'll learn the advantages of being a wise shopper. This much-needed advice will also enable you to better control the quality of your meals and the ingredients that go into them. I've even thrown in tips to help you stock your kitchen with all the supplies and equipment you'll need to get started.

And finally, there is a huge assortment of vegan recipes in this book to satisfy your appetite no matter what you're hungering for. That's right—you won't find any meat, eggs, dairy, or other animal products in any of these scrumptious dishes. The recipes contain ingredients from only plant-based sources, like fruits, vegetables, whole grains, and beans, including tofu and other soy-based products. So read on and get ready to make cooking, eating, and living as a single vegan a delicious, rewarding, and exciting experience!

Healthy, Wealthy, and Wise

e all want to live a long life and remain healthy. Unfortunately, the standard American diet (SAD), which is heavily based on animal products, has been linked to various chronic illnesses and diseases. Vegans, who consume no animal products at all, have significantly lower incidences of cancer, stroke, heart disease, kidney disease, diabetes, obesity, and arthritis than nonvegans. In general, they also have lower blood pressure and cholesterol levels and tend to be more physically fit than meat eaters, whom they often outlive by as much as ten years.

Most people are unaware that the human body doesn't require the milk or flesh of animals to remain healthy (with the exception of breast milk during infancy). Like many other species, all of our nutritional needs can be met through plant-based sources. Plant-based foods are generally low in sodium, calories, and saturated fats, and unlike animal-based foods, they contain absolutely no cholesterol. The following six classes of nutrients found in food provide the raw materials necessary for building and maintaining our bodies:

- water
- proteins
- carbohydrates
- vitamins
- minerals
- fats and oils

Plant-based foods also contain beneficial dietary fiber, which keeps us regular and helps our bodies eliminate toxins and maintain a proper weight. The Institute of Medicine, part of the National Academy of Sciences, recommends that we eat 14 grams of fiber for every 1,000 calories consumed. We can easily achieve this by eating lots of fruits, vegetables, and whole grains, and by purchasing high-fiber prepackaged products (check and compare the amounts listed on the product's nutrient panel).

Follow the rainbow to good health by eating red, yellow, orange, green, blue, and purple fruits and vegetables to ensure you're getting the widest variety of vital nutrients, flavors, and textures. The pigments that comprise these colors contain important antioxidants (substances that may reduce the risk of cancer and the progression of age-related diseases) and other phytonutrients (active compounds, found only in plants, that have health-promoting properties).

All living things, whether they're plants or animals, are made up of amino acids, which are the building blocks of protein. Our bodies naturally produce most of these, while the remainder, known as essential amino acids, must be obtained through the foods we eat. A vegan diet that incorporates a wide variety of wholesome foods will contain all of the essential amino acids required by the human body. Good choices include nuts and nut butters, sprouted seeds, leafy dark green vegetables, beans, soy-based products (such as tofu, tempeh, and soymilk), whole grains (like brown rice, amaranth, and quinoa), and sea vegetables (like nori, kelp, spirulina, and chlorella). It's a myth that vegan foods need to be eaten in certain combinations to create complete proteins (that is, proteins with all the essential amino acids in the proper proportions). Simply eating a variety of protein-rich plant foods throughout the day will result in a good balance of amino acids.

One nutrient that everyone (vegans and nonvegans alike) should be concerned about is vitamin B_{12}, even though just a small amount is needed for the formation of healthy blood cells and proper nerve functioning. However, undetected and untreated vitamin B_{12} deficiency can lead to anemia and permanent nerve and brain damage. Vitamin B_{12} is created through bacterial fermentation and is found in the intestines of animals (humans included) and in soil and water that is contaminated with this compound. Because we generally wash our fresh foods before eating them, and our public drinking water is filtered to remove harmful bacteria and other potentially dangerous organisms, there are no longer viable amounts of vitamin B_{12} available to us through these means. As a vegan, you can get all that you need by taking a 25 mg supplement once a week, eating foods that are fortified with vitamin B_{12}, and sprinkling a few tablespoons of Red Star Vegetarian Support Formula nutritional yeast on your food every day.

To address vegan and vegetarian nutritional needs, the Physicians Committee for Responsible Medicine (www.pcrm.org) has developed the plant-based New

Four Food Groups. Their guide is easy to follow and includes recommendations for all age groups. As you plan your meals, try to adhere to the basic guidelines outlined in table 1 (page 6).

Your caloric needs are determined by your age (teens need more calories than children and older adults), gender (men need more calories than women), height (taller people need more calories than shorter people), and physical activity level (athletes need more calories than sedentary and overweight people). For adults of average height, weight, and activity level, consuming 1,600 to 2,200 calories per day is recommended. Sadly, it's estimated that by the next decade nearly half of all American children and adults will be overweight or obese. If you're concerned about your weight, consult your doctor, become more active, and drop your daily caloric intake by 250 to 500 calories.

Smart eating habits are easier to learn and adapt to when you are young. To avoid becoming a statistic

- eat a variety of foods and make wise food choices;
- reduce your intake of excess salt, sugary sweets, refined grains, processed products, and high-fat foods whenever possible;
- increase the amount of dietary fiber you consume by eating more beans, fruits, and vegetables;
- drink eight or more eight-ounce glasses of water and other liquids throughout the day to stay properly hydrated;
- exercise and be physically active on a regular basis;
- get plenty of fresh air and sunshine.

If you're still concerned about your nutritional needs, then also do the following:

- occasionally take a vegan multivitamin and mineral supplement
- read food nutrition labels and compare brands when shopping (many breads, grains, cereals, soy-based products, beverages, and fruit juices, including orange juice, are fortified with important nutrients)

Remember, eating a vegan diet will make you healthy (vibrant, energetic, lighter, and leaner around the middle), wealthy (in fiber and vital nutrients), and wise (by reducing your risk of disease).

For additional information to support your health and diet, search the Internet and bookshelves for books and articles by respected vegan doctors and experts, such as Neal Barnard, John McDougall, Michael Klaper, Milton Mills, and T. Colin Campbell.

TABLE 1: Minimum Daily Guidelines for a Vegan Diet

Food Group	Minimum Daily Servings	Serving Size
GRAINS		
whole grains and products made from them (such as breads, pastas, and cereals)	5 servings	¾ to 1 cup ready-to-eat cereal ½ cup cooked cereal, whole grains, or pasta ½ bun or bagel 1 slice of bread
LEGUMES		
beans, nuts and seeds, nut and seed butters, vegan meat alternatives, and soy products	3 servings	1 cup soymilk ½ cup cooked legumes 4 ounces tofu or tempeh ¼ cup nuts or seeds 1 ounce vegan meat alternative 1 tablespoon nut or seed butter
FRUITS		
	3 servings	1 whole fruit (apple, pear, orange, banana, peach, plum) ½ cup frozen or cooked fruit ½ cup fruit juice ¼ cup dried fruit
VEGETABLES, dark green leafy		
broccoli, cabbage, collard greens, kale, spinach	2 to 3 servings	1 cup raw vegetables ½ cup cooked fresh or frozen vegetables
VEGETABLES, other		
	2 to 3 servings	1 cup raw vegetables ½ cup cooked fresh or frozen vegetables

Be a Smart Shopper

Consumers often forget that they ultimately control the market. Money talks, so use each dollar you spend to voice your ideals and express your concerns. Purchase from all-vegan companies whenever possible to show your opposition to animal cruelty. If shopping at large retailers, let them know there is a demand by requesting more sustainable, organic, and cruelty-free vegan merchandise. Here are a few other smart shopping tips.

Have a Game Plan

Some people like to plan out their meals, compile a list of needed ingredients, and then go shopping. Others prefer to check out in-store specials or let what's in season determine what they will purchase and prepare. Try combining these techniques by making a list of needed items, searching out incredible deals, and formulating ways to best use your purchases for several different meals. Systematically work through the aisles, starting with produce, then pantry staples and canned goods, and ending with refrigerated and frozen items (to avoid spoilage or thawing).

Read Labels

Become a diligent label reader and educate yourself about the many obscure and often "hidden" animal-derived ingredients. Compare brands to find the ones with the highest-quality ingredients and best value for your money, to avoid frustration and disappointment due to overspending or purchasing unsuitable products.

Go Organic

Countless toxic substances such as pesticides, herbicides, fertilizers, and hazardous wastes from animals, industries, and water treatment centers contaminate food crops and many of the other items we use. Supporting and buying organic products reduces or eliminates exposure for both workers and consumers and promotes sustainability, which is better for the environment (especially our soil and water supply) and the future of this planet.

Sure, some organic items cost more, but think of it as an investment in your health and the health of the planet. Try switching to organics one item or one cabinet at a time. Begin with fresh and frozen produce, as they often contain large amounts of pesticide and fertilizer residues, followed by bulk and prepackaged foods, and then cleaning products and health and beauty items.

Keep It Local

Support your local economy and community by buying from merchants, shops, and farmers markets in your area. Many goods travel one or two thousand miles or more before reaching consumers. You can help reduce the negative environmental effects of transporting products long distances, ensure that local farmers and business owners stay in business, and cut your final costs by choosing locally sourced goods over those shipped in from other areas.

Start Fresh

For the best nutritional value, choose fresh produce whenever possible and let these selections guide your other purchases and menu plans. To avoid spoilage, purchase smaller amounts that you know you will use. Dried herbs work fine in most recipes, but use fresh parsley and cilantro whenever possible, as their flavors are more vibrant and will liven up your dishes; the fresh herbs will also add visual appeal.

Shop in Season

Keep variety in your diet and stay on a budget by rotating your fruit and vegetable selections with the changing seasons. Foods are more flavorful if picked when ripe and ready, during their growing seasons, and not just rushed to market. Let your eyes guide you to the best deals and freshest quality ingredients. Don't worry about leaving empty-handed, as there are many commonly used varieties of fresh fruits and vegetables available year-round in most areas of the country.

Bulk Up

Whenever possible, buy items from bulk bins or dispensers, especially pantry staples like beans, nuts, seeds, flours, sugars, seasonings, oils, and vinegars. Bulk items are usually fresher and less expensive, and you can purchase the exact quantity you want or need. Buying in bulk is also an environmentally friendly way to shop, because less manufacturer's packaging is required and wasted; you simply place your purchases in brown paper bags, recyclable plastic bags, or even your own containers.

Store Your Stash

To avoid spills and pest infestations, use airtight containers or zipper-lock plastic bags to store ingredients that will be kept at room temperature. (To reduce your reliance on petrochemical products and prevent them from going into landfills, minimize the use of plastic bags and wash and reuse them whenever feasible.) Be sure to keep these items in a cool, dry place or cabinet, away from heat and direct sunlight. Liquid sweeteners (such as maple syrup and agave nectar) and items with a high oil content (such as nuts and seeds) can spoil very quickly and are best stored in the refrigerator, where they will keep for several weeks or months. Alternatively, you can extend their shelf life by freezing them for several months or up to a year. Dried fruits remain soft and fresh when stored in airtight containers; keep them either in a cool, dry place or in the refrigerator.

Taking Stock: Pantry Essentials

tocking your cabinets, fridge, and freezer with these suggested staples will make cooking and baking for one a snap. Many of these ingredients are used in the recipes in this book. You may also want to keep additional items like coffee or tea, crackers, popcorn, tortilla chips, and other snacks and favorite foods on hand to satisfy your meal and munching needs.

Baking Staples

- aluminum-free baking powder
- baking soda
- chocolate or carob chips (optional)
- cocoa powder and/or carob powder
- coconut, unsweetened shredded dried (optional)
- flours and starches (such as arrowroot, barley flour, cornmeal, cornstarch, whole grain spelt flour, whole wheat pastry flour, and vital wheat gluten)
- sweeteners, dry (such as beet sugar, maple sugar, turbinado sugar, unbleached cane sugar, and vegan powdered sugar)
- sweeteners, liquid (such as agave nectar, brown rice syrup, maple syrup, and molasses)

Dry Goods and Bulk Items

- beans, dried (such as black beans, black-eyed peas, chickpeas, green split peas, kidney beans, lentils, navy beans, pinto beans, and red beans)
- fruit, dried (such as apricots, banana chips, cherries, cranberries, currants, dates, figs, and raisins)

- grains, whole (such as barley, bulgur, millet, oats, quinoa, and rice)
- nuts, raw (such as almonds, Brazil nuts, cashews, hazelnuts, pecans, pine nuts, pistachios, and walnuts)
- pastas, whole grain (such as whole wheat couscous and whole wheat, spelt, or brown rice noodles in various shapes and sizes)
- seeds, raw (such as hemp seeds, flaxseeds, poppy seeds, pumpkin seeds, sesame seeds, and sunflower seeds)
- sun-dried tomato pieces

Canned, Boxed, and Bottled Items

- beans (such as black beans, black-eyed peas, cannellini beans, chickpeas, kidney beans, lentils, mixed beans, navy beans, pinto beans, and red beans)
- breadcrumbs, dry (packaged in bags, boxes, and canisters)
- cereal, ready to eat (such as bran flakes, crispy brown rice, puffed grains, and shredded wheat)
- condiments, bottled or jarred (such as barbecue sauce, Dijon mustard, hot sauce, ketchup, pickles, relish, salad dressings, salsa, vegan mayonnaise, and whole grain and yellow mustard)
- coconut milk, canned (lite or full fat)
- fruit, canned (such as apples, cherries, oranges, peaches, pears, and pineapple)
- fruit jams and jellies (such as apricot, blackberry, grape, orange marmalade, raspberry, and strawberry)
- fruit juices, bottled or frozen (such as apple, cherry, cranberry, grape, orange, peach, pear, pineapple, and raspberry)
- nut and seed butters (such as almond, cashew, and peanut butter, and tahini)
- vegetable broth (instant cubes or powder, or liquid in cans or aseptic boxes)
- vegetables, canned (such as beets, corn kernels, peas, pumpkin purée, sauerkraut, and mixed vegetables)
- tomato products, canned (such as crushed tomatoes, diced tomatoes, marinara sauce, pasta sauce, tomato juice, tomato paste, tomato sauce, and tomato-vegetable juice blends)

Seasonings and Flavorings

- herbs, dried (such as basil, dill, Italian seasoning blend, marjoram, oregano, rosemary, sage, tarragon, and thyme)
- flavoring extracts (such as almond, coconut, peppermint, and vanilla)

- nutritional yeast flakes
- oils (such as flavored oils, flaxseed oil, hemp seed oil, olive oil, safflower oil, and toasted sesame oil)
- sea salt
- spices, ground (such as allspice, cardamom, cayenne, chili powder, cinnamon, cloves, coriander, cumin, curry powder, fennel, garlic powder, ginger, onion powder, paprika, turmeric, and white pepper)
- spices, whole (such as peppercorns and nutmeg)
- tamari
- vinegars (such as apple cider vinegar, balsamic vinegar, brown rice vinegar, flavored vinegars, and red wine vinegar)

Alternatives to Animal Products

- dairy alternatives (such as nondairy cream cheese, nondairy sour cream, nonhydrogenated vegan margarine, soymilk and other nondairy milks, vegan cheese blocks and slices, and vegan Parmesan)
- vegan meat alternatives (such as regular and silken tofu, seitan, tempeh, vegan burger crumbles, vegan deli slices, vegan meatballs, and veggie burgers and dogs)

Fresh, Refrigerated, and Frozen Foods

- bread products, whole grain (such as corn and flour tortillas, bagels, English muffins, loaves, and pita bread)
- fruits, fresh in season (such as apples, bananas, blueberries, cherries, mangoes, oranges, peaches, raspberries, and strawberries)
- fruits, frozen (such as blueberries, cherries, mixed berries and mixed fruit blends, peaches, raspberries, and strawberries)
- herbs and seasonings, fresh (such as basil, cilantro, garlic, ginger, parsley, and prepared horseradish)
- juice concentrates, frozen (such as apple, cranberry, and orange)
- treats, frozen (such as juice bars and other novelties, nondairy ice creams, and sorbets)
- vegetables, fresh in season (such as Asian eggplants, avocados, beets, cabbages, carrots, celery, green onions, leafy greens, lettuces, mixed baby greens, peppers, potatoes, onions, radishes, and spinach)
- vegetables, frozen (such as broccoli, corn kernels, cauliflower, edamame, green beans, mixed vegetable combinations, peas, and spinach)

Gearing Up: Useful Equipment

f you want to cook and bake like the pros, and enjoy easier and less stressful meal preparations, then equip your kitchen with the proper gear, gadgets, and gizmos. Purchase items as your budget allows and look for prepackaged sets for the best deals.

Kitchen Basics

- **airtight storage containers**

  To store dry goods, bulk ingredients, and leftovers in the refrigerator or freezer, or for transporting food items, select high-quality containers made of glass or plastic.

- **baking pans and cookie sheets**

  For oven baking, select nonaluminum metal pans.

  - two 10 x 15-inch or larger cookie sheets
  - two 8- or 9-inch round pie pans
  - one 8- or 9-inch square pan
  - one 8 x 4 x 2½-inch loaf pan
  - one 9 x 13-inch rectangular pan
  - one 8- or 9-inch springform pan for vegan cheesecakes and other desserts

- **colander**

  Use a large, plastic or metal colander to wash fresh produce and dried beans, and for straining liquids and draining pasta.

- **cookware**

  For stovetop cooking, select pots and pans with matching, tight-fitting lids. Stainless steel pans with metal handles are a wise choice and also oven safe. Nonstick or anodized aluminum pans are easy to clean and require less oil to prevent sticking, but you will need to use wooden or plastic utensils to avoid scratching them.

  - one 1-quart saucepan
  - one 2-quart saucepan
  - one 4-quart saucepan
  - one 6-quart pot
  - one 6- or 8-inch skillet
  - one 10-inch skillet

- **cutting boards**

  Purchase thick, hardwood cutting boards. The minimum size should be at least 8 inches square; but for greater versatility and to accomplish most tasks, 10 x 15 inches or larger would be ideal. Use lemon juice or vinegar to remove any stubborn stains and sanitize them.

  - one or more cutting boards for vegetables and strong-flavored foods (such as onions)
  - one or more cutting boards for fruits, breads, baked goods, and mild-flavored foods

- **knives**

  A knife set is a good investment, but just a few knives are essential.

  - one chef's knife with a 6- to 10-inch blade and a sturdy handle to chop, dice, slice, and mince
  - one serrated knife with an 8-inch blade to slice bread, desserts, tomatoes, and vegan cheeses
  - one small utility or paring knife with a 3- to 5-inch blade to peel and cut fruits and small foods

- **linens (dish cloths and towels), sponges, and scrub pads**

  Use dish cloths, sponges, and scrub pads for washing and scrubbing dishes, cookware, and bakeware, for cleaning counters and work surfaces, and for catching drips and spills. Cloth towels are more environmentally friendly than paper towels for drying dishes and hands. To protect clothing during meal preparation, wear an apron or tuck a towel into your collar or waistband.

- **measuring cups**

  - one set for dry ingredients, including $\frac{1}{4}$-cup, $\frac{1}{3}$-cup, $\frac{1}{2}$-cup, and 1-cup sizes
  - one 2-cup or 4-cup capacity for liquid ingredients

- **measuring spoons**

  - one set for dry ingredients
  - one set for wet ingredients

- **mixing bowls**

  Purchase attractive bowls made of metal, glass, or plastic, in various sizes (ideally with matching lids), that can be used for both mixing and serving.

- **oven mitts and potholders**

  Use oven mitts or potholders to prevent burns from hot pans, handles, and cookware edges, and when removing items from the oven. Purchase thick, well-insulated cloth mitts or potholders or high-temperature, heat-resistant, silicone varieties, and discard any ripped or damaged ones to avoid injuries.

- **ovenproof cookware**

  For baking, choose ceramic, glass, or nonaluminum metal casserole dishes in various sizes, ideally with matching, tight-fitting lids. Casserole dishes are versatile because they allow you to cook on the stovetop, bake, reheat, serve, and store foods using the same container.

- **strainer**

  Use a fine-mesh strainer for rinsing whole grains, straining liquids, or sifting flour and other ingredients for baking.

- **utensils**

  Utensils are used for both preparing and serving foods. Choose ones made from metal, wood, plastic, or silicone.

  - one long-handled fork, for piercing foods or, when paired with a large spoon, to serve pasta or salad
  - a variety of solid spoons
  - one or more slotted spoons
  - one ladle
  - one pair of tongs
  - one potato masher
  - one whisk
  - one metal or heatproof flat spatula for flipping and serving foods
  - one or more rubber spatulas for mixing ingredients and scraping the sides of containers

Machines and Gadgets

- **blender**

  A blender is used to chop, mix, whip, and emulsify ingredients quickly. Select either a classic upright or handheld immersion model, which can blend ingredients directly in the mixing bowl or saucepan.

- **can opener**

  A can opener is essential for opening canned goods. Select either an electric or hand-cranked model (newer hand-cranked openers are available with extra safety features).

- **food processor**

  Food processors mix, blend, and emulsify ingredients. They are more efficient than a blender for mixing stiff dough and batters and for coarsely or finely chopping items. Many models also include attachments for slicing and shredding.

- **grater**

  Choose either the classic box style or a handheld model to finely or coarsely grate, shred, and slice food items.

- **kitchen timer**

  A kitchen timer will help you to keep track of exact cooking and baking times to ensure more consistent results. Select either a hand-cranked or digital model.

- **oil brush or mister**

  A brush (made from synthetic fiber or silicone) or mister (special non-aerosol spray bottles designed specifically for misting oil) will allow you to lightly coat pans with your oil of choice. By using these tools instead of conventional cooking oil sprays, you can avoid the inferior oils and harmful propellants these products often contain.

- **peppermill**

  Freshly ground pepper has the best flavor. Peppermills are available in various styles and sizes and are used to finely or coarsely grind whole peppercorns.

- **reamer or citrus juicer**

  Manual reamers and electric citrus juicers are ridged, teardrop-shaped devices used to extract the juice from lemons, limes, and oranges.

- **steamer basket**

  A steamer basket is used in combination with a large pot or skillet for wilting or steaming vegetables or other foods. Select either a bamboo steamer or a collapsible metal basket that is inserted into a pot of simmering water. Alternatively, purchase a multipurpose pasta pot consisting of a large pot with a matching lid, an offset large steamer-strainer pot insert, and often a smaller steamer basket insert.

- **toaster or toaster oven**

  A toaster is primarily used for toasting bread. A toaster oven can also be used for reheating cooked food, heating frozen entrées, and light baking.

- **vegetable brush**

  A sturdy bristled brush should be used to remove debris from unpeeled fruits and vegetables. To avoid cross-contamination (the process of carrying bacteria from one object to another object), don't clean your sink, pots, or pans with the same brush you use to clean your produce.

- **vegetable peeler**

  A vegetable peeler is a handy tool that removes skins and imperfections from fruits and vegetables and can be used to make thin slices or decorations, such as vegetable "noodles" and chocolate shavings.

- **zester**

  A zester is a handheld tool that safely and quickly removes fine, thin strips of peel from citrus fruits or vegetables. It can also be used to make decorative edges on food.

Grooving with Whole Grains

Cooking grains is as easy as boiling water. All varieties are rich in fiber and protein, and they are an excellent value because they double or triple in volume after cooking. And if that isn't enough to tempt you, the icing on the cake is that many can be prepared in under thirty minutes. Exact cooking times depend on the size of the grain. Smaller or refined grains (such as millet and quinoa) cook more quickly, and larger whole grains (such as rice or wheat berries) take longer. Grains can be found in the bulk bins of natural food stores and prepackaged. They are sold individually or as mixed blends and are available plain, seasoned, or with added ingredients, such as dried vegetables.

Tips for Achieving Grain Perfection

Here are some suggestions to help you groove with grains:

- Avoid mushy grains by measuring water and grains accurately.
- Combine the water or cooking liquid, grain, salt, and any seasonings in a medium or large pot with a tight-fitting lid. Bring to a boil over high heat, cover, reduce the heat to low heat, and cook for the required time (see table 2, page 17).
- Accurately monitor the cooking time by using a kitchen timer or watch.
- Avoid lifting the lid as the grain cooks; only check it quickly after the allotted cooking time has expired. Remove the cooked grain from the heat and let it rest in the covered pot for 5 to 10 minutes. This will give it a little extra time to steam. Fluff or stir the grain with a fork and serve.
- If at the end of the cooking time the grain is tender but some liquid remains in the pot, just drain it off.

TABLE 2: Cooking Guide for Common Grains

Grain (1 cup dry)	Cooking Liquid (in cups)	Cooking Time and/or Method	Yield
Amaranth	2 cups	25 to 30 minutes	2 to 2 ½ cups
Barley (pearled or hulled)	3 ½ cups	50 to 55 minutes	3 ½ cups
Buckwheat groats (kasha)	2 cups	May be toasted prior to cooking; cook for 15 to 20 minutes	2 to 2 ½ cups
Bulgur	2 cups	Place bulgur in a heatproof bowl and pour boiling water over it. Cover and let rest for 25 to 30 minutes.	3 cups
Couscous	2 cups	Place couscous in a heatproof bowl and pour boiling water over it. Cover and let rest for 5 minutes.	3 cups
Millet	2 cups	May be toasted prior to cooking; cook for 25 to 35 minutes	3 ½ cups
Mixed grain blends	2 cups (or amount listed on package directions)	40 to 50 minutes	3 cups
Polenta (corn grits)	3 to 4 cups*	Bring the liquid to a boil in a pot and very slowly stir in the polenta. Cook over low heat, stirring often, for 20 to 30 minutes or until thickened and soft.	3 to 4 cups
Quinoa	2 cups	10 to 15 minutes	3 cups
Rice, basmati brown	2 cups	25 to 35 minutes	3 cups
Rice, basmati white	1¾ cups	15 to 20 minutes	3 cups
Rice, jasmine	1½ cups	15 to 20 minutes	3 cups
Rice, long-grain brown	2 cups	35 to 40 minutes	3 cups
Rice, short-grain brown	2 cups	40 to 45 minutes	3 cups
Rice, wild	2 cups (or amount listed on package directions)	35 to 40 minutes	3 cups
Rice, wild and brown blends	2 cups (or amount listed on package directions)	35 to 40 minutes	3 cups
Spelt berries	3 cups	1½ to 2 hours	2 ½ cups
Wheat berries	3 cups	1½ to 2 hours	2 ½ cups

* The smaller amount of liquid will make a thicker polenta; the larger amount will make a creamier polenta.

Flavor Boosters

- Before cooking grains, toast them in a dry pan until they are just a shade darker. This will impart a nutty flavor and help the grains cook faster.

- For extra flavor and color, use vegetable stock or fruit juice instead of water, or add a little tomato paste or other vegetable purée to the cooking liquid.

- Season grains with salt, ground pepper, dried herbs, and/or your favorite spices prior to cooking to release more of their flavors. Fresh herbs and citrus zest are best added at the end of the cooking time or just before serving.

- To make a pilaf, toast uncooked grains in a little oil until they are just a shade or two darker. This adds a nutty flavor and helps the grains retain their shape when they are cooked. If you like, toast the grains in oil with fresh garlic, onions, ginger, or finely chopped vegetables.

- For extra flavor, texture, and color contrast, and to turn plain grains into a heartier meal or side dish, add chopped vegetables, dried fruits, and/or nuts before or after the grains are cooked.

Culinary Creativity

hat's your approach to meals? Do you like to keep it simple? Perhaps you have a piece of fruit and toast or a smoothie for breakfast, and a soup-salad-sandwich combo, a bowl of beans and rice, or a pasta dish for lunch and dinner. Are you a grab-and-go grazer who likes easy, quick fixes and the instant gratification of just opening a package, can, or box? Maybe you are an aspiring gourmet who loves to cook everything from scratch, often prepares multiple-course meals, and creatively utilizes leftovers for other meals.

If you're a busy single cooking for one, combine approaches. Do more cooking on weekends and less during the week, use leftovers for other meals, preplan and use shortcut tricks, and make the most of both fresh and prepackaged ingredients. Effortlessly, you'll enjoy delicious, healthful meals rather than heating up a frozen pizza or ordering takeout.

Your kitchen endeavors should be pleasant and rewarding experiences, not chores or catastrophic events. Making a meal or a batch of cookies can be a lot of fun. Even if your first attempts flop or have mixed results, don't let it throw you; this often happens when trying out anything new. Remember, practice does make perfect. Using equipment like a blender, oven, or stovetop may seem scary at first, but this fear will fade after a few uses.

For the most success with your meals, start simple by preparing recipes using only a few ingredients and gradually build your culinary expertise before attempting more complicated recipes. Once you have mastered a few vegan recipes, show off your skills by sharing your vegan creations with others.

Helpful Culinary Tips

Here are some helpful preplanning tips and advice to help you become the master of your own kitchen and make cooking for one easier:

- Follow a recipe exactly as it is written the first time you make it.
- Prepare a recipe successfully several times before experimenting or making changes to it.
- Replace the same amount of one vegetable or fruit for another in recipes, as this rarely affects the outcome.
- Cut a recipe in half if it yields more than you can use. Write down your calculations and double-check them to avoid mistakes or wasting food or ingredients.
- Cook larger amounts of your favorite dried beans and grains than you need for a meal. They'll keep for several days in the refrigerator. Alternatively, freeze them in individual portions for later use.
- Precut the vegetables you use most often (such as carrots, celery, onions, or garlic) and store them in airtight containers in the refrigerator. They'll keep for several days.
- Juice several lemons, limes, or oranges at a time and store the juice in a covered container in the refrigerator. Freshly squeezed citrus juice (rather than jarred or canned) tastes best and will keep for several days. Alternatively, pour one or two tablespoons of juice as desired into ice cube trays, freeze until solid, and then transfer the frozen cubes to an airtight container and store them in the freezer.
- By more fresh ginger than you need for one recipe, as it will keep for two weeks in the refrigerator. Alternatively, store fresh ginger in the freezer in an airtight container and grate or chop it as needed, directly from the freezer.
- Buy prewashed and bagged greens, lettuces, and salad mixes, as well as packaged sprouts, to save time. They are great for sandwiches or wraps, as the base for a quick salad, or for extending leftover vegetables, grains, or pasta dishes.
- Use up leftover meals or ingredients by incorporating them into salads, stir-fries, soups, or casseroles.

- Drain canned beans in a colander and rinse them under running water to remove excess salt.
- Add fresh greens, whole grains, or beans to meals for extra fiber and protein.
- Choose nutritious snacks like fresh fruits and vegetables over chips and sweets.
- Cut the fat content of your meals by using an oil mister to coat your pans and bakeware. Replace all or part of the oil in a savory recipe with water or vegetable broth. Replace up to one-third of the amount of fat or margarine used in baked goods with applesauce, mashed bananas, or other fruit purées.

Ready, Set, Go!

Still a bit frightened or intimidated by your kitchen? Help has arrived! In the pages ahead, you'll find over one hundred recipes encompassing a wide variety of foods and cuisines, enough to cover all of your meal options from breakfast to dinner, not to mention some delicious desserts and sweet treats. So there's no way you'll get bored or find yourself eating the same old thing.

There are selections to fit every skill level and schedule, from the quick and easy using few ingredients or gadgets to the more involved, which require a little more time or effort. Each one yields only a few servings, allowing for a leftover or two, so you won't be overwhelmed having to constantly cook a new vegan meal every day for yourself. The recipes use fresh, frozen, and prepackaged ingredients, but feel free to substitute other ingredients as you like or to save time.

So are you ready to get started? Roll up your sleeves, get into the kitchen, and be fearless. In no time you'll be enjoying your very own vegan feasts. Prepare to express your vegan culinary creativity!

SAMPLES

SAMPLEMUS

21

One Week to a New World

ere is a week of sample menus to provide you with ideas for planning your meals. It incorporates the daily dietary recommendations of the New Four Food Groups and illustrates how simple it really is to fulfill all of your nutritional needs with very little effort.

DAY 1

Breakfast
- Maple-Pecan French Toast (page 33) topped with maple syrup and sliced fruit or berries
- fruit juice, nondairy milk, coffee, or tea

Lunch
- baked potato with toppings of choice
- tossed salad with dressing of choice

Dinner
- Bandito Burritos (page 68)
- cooked grain of choice
- tortilla chips and salsa

Treat
- scoops of nondairy ice cream or sorbet topped with sliced fruit or berries

DAY 2

Breakfast
- hot oatmeal made with nondairy milk topped with your choice of flaxseeds, nuts, seeds, sliced fruit, or berries
- fruit juice, coffee, or tea

Lunch
- Health-Nut Heroes (page 66)
- piece of fresh fruit

Dinner
- Baked Ziti Casserole (page 85)
- steamed vegetables or tossed salad with dressing of choice
- whole grain bread or roll

Treat
- Old-Fashioned Vanilla Pudding and Pie Filling (page 132) topped with toasted coconut or sliced fruit or berries

DAY 3

Breakfast
- cold breakfast cereal with nondairy milk topped with sliced fruit or berries
- fruit juice, coffee, or tea

Lunch
- Maple-Mustard Pasta Salad (page 60) on mixed greens
- piece of fresh fruit

Dinner
- Tex-Mex Bean Burgers (page 76) on whole grain bun or bread with toppings and condiments of choice
- cut fresh vegetables
- tortilla chips and salsa, or potato chips

Treat
- Crispy Rice Cereal Treats (page 134)

DAY 4

Breakfast
- Hearty Breakfast Skillet (page 36)
- toasted whole grain bread or English muffin
- fruit juice, nondairy milk, coffee, or tea

Lunch
- canned vegan soup or chili
- whole grain crackers
- piece of fresh fruit

Dinner
- Pita Margherita (page 73)
- tossed salad with dressing of choice

Treat
- Rich Dark Chocolate Cake (page 120) dusted with vegan powdered sugar and topped with sliced fruit or berries

DAY 5

Breakfast
- Nana Nutter Roll-Ups (page 62)
- fruit juice, nondairy milk, coffee, or tea

Lunch
- A Gigantic Garden Salad Bowl (page 56)
- whole grain crackers
- piece of fresh fruit

Dinner
- vegan hot dog on whole grain bun or bread with toppings and condiments of choice
- canned vegetarian baked beans
- cut fresh vegetables

Treat
- Frozen Yogurt Berry Pops (page 127)

DAY 6

Breakfast
- Fruit and Granola Parfait (page 31) or fresh fruit salad
- toasted whole grain bagel or English muffin topped with nut butter of choice
- fruit juice, nondairy milk, coffee, or tea

Lunch
- Golden Vegetable Noodle Soup (page 51)
- grilled cheese sandwich made with whole grain bread and slices of vegan cheese
- cut fresh vegetables

Dinner
- Sizzling Sesame Stir-Fry (page 80)
- cooked grain of choice

Treat
- scoops of nondairy ice cream or sorbet topped with sliced fruit or berries

DAY 7

Breakfast
- Hacienda Home Fries (page 35)
- toasted whole grain bread or English muffin topped with fruit jelly or nut butter of choice
- fruit juice, nondairy milk, coffee, or tea

Lunch
- sandwich on whole grain bread made with vegan deli slices, slice of vegan cheese, and toppings and condiments of choice
- cut fresh vegetables
- piece of fresh fruit

Dinner
- Eggplant and Chickpea Stew (page 94)
- cooked grain or pasta of choice

Treat
- Orange-Spiced Oatmeal Raisin Cookies (page 115)

RECIPES

Great Starts
breakfast and more

It's no wonder that breakfast is considered the most important meal of the day. After sleeping for many hours (hopefully close to eight), your body desperately needs fuel to get your motor running. The following recipes will provide you with all of the necessary energy and nutrition to get your day off to a great start. If you're short on time and need something to grab and go, make one of the beverage or smoothie recipes or perhaps a colorful breakfast parfait to take along with you. On days when you're less rushed, find yourself hankering for a hearty feast, or just want to make something special, give the vegan sausages, flapjacks, French toast, or tasty skillet-cooked breakfasts a try.

Similar in taste to bottled brands, this spicy beverage based on tomatoes and vegetables is a quick and easy way to get more raw food into your daily diet. Hot sauce and horseradish give it extra zip.

spicy Vegetable Cocktail

YIELD: 1½ CUPS

1½ cups diced plum tomatoes

¼ cup diced green bell peppers

¼ cup diced red bell peppers

¼ cup diced celery

1 green onion, thinly sliced
(about 2 tablespoons)

1½ teaspoons freshly squeezed lemon juice

½ teaspoon prepared horseradish

Sea salt

Freshly ground black pepper

Hot sauce

Place the tomatoes, bell peppers, celery, green onion, lemon juice, and horseradish in a blender and process for 1 to 2 minutes or until completely smooth. Season with salt, pepper, and hot sauce to taste and blend again briefly. Serve immediately in a tall glass, plain or over ice.

VARIATIONS

- Use other raw vegetables of your choice.
- Add a handful of chopped fresh herbs.

Sipping on a smoothie is a great way to get two to three servings of fruit in a single glass. This creamy, golden smoothie is made with a sweet and flavorful blend of fruits, soymilk, and orange juice. It's guaranteed to bring a smile to your face as you welcome a new day.

Sunrise **smoothie**

YIELD: 2 CUPS

1 medium banana, sliced (about ¾ cup)

1 medium mango, diced (about ½ cup)

½ cup pineapple chunks

½ cup soymilk or other nondairy milk of choice

Juice of 1 medium orange (about ⅓ cup)

Place all of the ingredients in a blender and process for 1 to 2 minutes or until completely smooth. Serve immediately in a tall glass with a straw.

VARIATIONS

- Substitute other fresh or frozen fruits or juice to suit your tastes.
- Replace the soymilk and orange juice with an equal amount of filtered water or other liquid of choice.

Mixing greens and berries may give this beverage an odd color, but don't let that stop you from enjoying it as a refreshing morning pick-me-up. It's a powerful combination that is rich in antioxidants, fiber, and protein. It will make you feel energized and ready to tackle anything.

berry Power Shake

YIELD: 2 CUPS

1 cup fresh or frozen berries of choice or mixed berries

1 leaf green or purple kale, stemmed and torn into pieces (about ¾ cup)

½ cup filtered water

½ cup ice cubes

2 pitted dates

2 Brazil nuts, or ¼ cup other nuts of choice

Place all of the ingredients in a blender and process for 1 to 2 minutes or until completely smooth. Serve immediately in a tall glass with a straw.

TIP: Boost the nutritional value of this shake by adding a handful of flaxseeds or hemp seeds to the blender prior to processing.

This fresh fruit treat is as pretty to look at as it is delicious to eat. It's made with generous layers of fresh fruit and berries, granola, and soy yogurt flavored with bananas. It's presented in a similar fashion to an ice cream sundae. Breakfast treat or dessert, you choose.

Fruit and Granola **parfait**

YIELD: 1 LARGE SERVING

1 medium banana, thinly sliced (about ¾ cup)

1 kiwi, peeled, quartered lengthwise, and sliced (about ½ cup)

⅓ cup blueberries

⅓ cup sliced strawberries

1 container (6 ounces) **plain or vanilla soy yogurt**

1 cup granola

Divide the banana evenly between two small bowls and set one bowl aside. Add the kiwi, blueberries, and strawberries, stir gently to combine, and set aside. Using a fork, mash the reserved banana slices, keeping them a bit chunky. Add the soy yogurt and stir until well combined.

To assemble the parfait, layer half of the fruit mixture, half of the granola, and half of the yogurt mixture in the bottom of a large glass or bowl. Repeat the layering procedure with the remaining fruit, granola, and yogurt mixture. Serve immediately.

VARIATIONS

- Substitute other flavors of soy yogurt and varieties of fresh berries or fruit to suit your own personal tastes.
- For an extra-special treat, replace the banana and soy yogurt mixture with an equal amount of nondairy ice cream or sorbet.

These flapjacks, also known as pancakes, made with soured soymilk and a touch of cinnamon and vanilla, will remind you of the ones your mom used to make (or ones you wish she had made). They cook up light and fluffy without the use of eggs or dairy products. Serve them with your choice of margarine, jam or preserves, fresh fruit or berries, maple syrup, or Berry Fruit Sauce or Syrup (page 124).

fabulous Flapjacks

YIELD: 4 PANCAKES (2 SERVINGS)

⅔ cup soymilk or other nondairy milk of choice

1 tablespoon freshly squeezed lemon juice or apple cider vinegar

⅔ cup whole wheat pastry flour

1½ teaspoons unbleached cane sugar or beet sugar

½ teaspoon ground cinnamon

½ teaspoon aluminum-free baking powder

¼ teaspoon baking soda

¼ teaspoon sea salt

1 tablespoon safflower oil

½ teaspoon vanilla extract

Place the soymilk and lemon juice in a small bowl and stir to combine. Set aside for 10 minutes to thicken.

Place the flour, sugar, cinnamon, baking powder, baking soda, and salt in a medium bowl and whisk them together. Pour the thickened soymilk mixture, safflower oil, and vanilla extract into the dry ingredients, whisk well to combine, and set the batter aside for 5 minutes.

Lightly oil a large skillet and place it over medium heat. When the skillet is hot, use a ⅓-cup measuring cup to portion the batter into the skillet for each flapjack. Cook for 2 to 3 minutes or until the edges of the flapjacks are slightly dry and bubbles appear on top. Flip the flapjacks over with a metal or heatproof spatula and cook for 2 to 3 minutes or until golden brown on other side. Lightly oil the skillet again and repeat the cooking procedure for the remaining batter. Serve hot with your desired toppings.

VARIATIONS

Add other ingredients to the flapjack batter, such as sliced fresh fruit, fresh or frozen berries, chopped nuts, ground flaxseeds, or chocolate or carob chips. Alternatively, sprinkle the additions of your choice on top of the batter as the flapjacks cook.

Just because you avoid dairy products and eggs doesn't mean you have to give up French toast. Pecans, maple syrup, and spices contribute to a creamy and flavorful mixture that transforms humble slices of bread into a magnificent breakfast. Serve it with your choice of margarine, jam, maple syrup, sliced fresh fruit, berries, or Berry Fruit Sauce or Syrup (page 124).

Maple-Pecan french toast

YIELD: 2 SLICES (1 SERVING)

¼ cup pecans

¼ cup filtered water

3 tablespoons maple syrup

½ teaspoon vanilla extract

¼ teaspoon ground cinnamon

⅛ teaspoon ground ginger

⅛ teaspoon sea salt

2 slices whole grain bread of choice

Process the pecans in a blender or food processor for 1 minute until they are finely ground. Add the water, maple syrup, vanilla extract, cinnamon, ginger, and salt and process for 1 minute or until smooth and creamy.

Place the bread slices in a large casserole dish and pour the pecan mixture over them. Flip the bread over to coat the other side. Allow the slices to soak in the mixture for 1 minute.

Lightly oil a large skillet and place it over medium heat. When the skillet is hot, carefully place the soaked bread slices in it and cook them for 1 to 2 minutes or until golden brown on the bottom. Flip the slices over with a metal or heatproof spatula and cook for 1 to 2 minutes or until golden brown on the other side. Serve hot with your desired toppings.

These spicy tempeh patties require a bit more time to prepare than prepackaged ones, but they taste better and are well worth the extra effort. Enjoy the patties as a side dish or sandwich filling, or cube or crumble the cooked patties and add them to sauces, casseroles, pasta, or grain dishes, or use them as a topping for pizza.

sweet Italian "Sausages"

YIELD: 4 SAUSAGES (2 SERVINGS)

8 ounces tempeh

⅓ cup whole wheat flour or spelt flour

1 tablespoon thinly sliced green onion

1½ teaspoons tamari

1½ teaspoons balsamic vinegar

1½ teaspoons maple syrup

1½ teaspoons olive oil

1½ teaspoons minced garlic

1 teaspoon Italian seasoning blend

½ teaspoon ground fennel

½ teaspoon crushed red pepper flakes

⅛ teaspoon freshly ground black pepper

Crumble the tempeh into a small bowl using your fingers. Add all of the remaining ingredients and stir until well combined.

Use a ⅓-cup measuring cup to portion each sausage patty by lightly filling and gently packing the tempeh mixture into the measuring cup with the back of a spoon. Flip the measuring cup over onto a large plate and give it a tap to release the mixture. Form each portion into a patty and chill them in the refrigerator for 30 minutes.

Lightly oil a large skillet and place it over medium heat. Arrange the patties in the hot skillet and cook them for 5 to 7 minutes or until golden brown on the bottom. Flip the patties over with a metal or heatproof spatula and cook for 5 minutes longer or until golden brown on the other side and crisp around the edges. Add additional olive oil to the skillet, if needed, to prevent the patties from sticking. Serve hot.

TIP: These sausage patties can be made in larger batches, precooked, and frozen in an airtight container for up to 3 months. When you are ready to use them, simply reheat the frozen patties in the oven or a skillet.

Here is a Tex-Mex twist on classic home-fried potatoes. This recipe is made with a colorful and tasty combination of yams, corn, zucchini, peppers, and seasonings, all cooked up together in a skillet. Serve it as a breakfast side dish or as a filling for a breakfast burrito or wrap, or combine it with grains for a hearty main dish. You can also enjoy it as a chunky dip, topped with salsa and served with tortilla chips or crackers.

hacienda Home Fries

YIELD: 2 TO 3 SERVINGS

1 large garnet yam, peeled, quartered lengthwise, and sliced

2 teaspoons olive oil

¾ cup diced yellow or red onions

1 cup diced zucchini

½ cup fresh or frozen corn kernels

½ cup diced red bell peppers

½ cup diced green bell peppers

1 medium jalapeño chile, seeded and finely diced

⅓ cup thinly sliced green onions

¼ cup chopped fresh cilantro or parsley

1 tablespoon minced garlic

1 teaspoon chili powder

½ teaspoon ground cumin

½ teaspoon sea salt

¼ teaspoon freshly ground black pepper

Place the yams and olive oil in a large skillet and cook over medium heat for 5 minutes, stirring often. Add the onions, zucchini, corn, bell peppers, and chile and cook and stir for 5 minutes. Add all of the remaining ingredients and cook and stir for 3 to 5 minutes or until the vegetables are fork-tender. Serve hot.

VARIATION

Add ½ cup canned black or red beans to the mixture as it cooks.

Provide your body with plenty of energy to make it through a hectic day with this savory mixture of tempeh, onions, carrots, and the green cousins broccoli and kale. Serve it with slices of fresh fruit or whole grain toast.

hearty Breakfast Skillet

YIELD: 2 SERVINGS

4 ounces tempeh, cut into ½-inch cubes

2 teaspoons olive oil

1½ cups small broccoli florets

½ cup diced yellow onions

½ cup diced carrots

2 leaves kale, stemmed and chopped (about 1½ cups)

¼ cup chopped pitted olives of choice

1 tablespoon minced garlic

1 tablespoon tamari

1 tablespoon nutritional yeast flakes

1 teaspoon dried basil or Italian seasoning blend

¼ teaspoon sea salt

⅛ teaspoon freshly ground black pepper

Place the tempeh and olive oil in a large skillet and cook over medium heat for 2 minutes, stirring often. Add the broccoli, onions, and carrots and cook and stir for 3 minutes. Add all of the remaining ingredients and cook and stir for 2 to 3 minutes longer or until the kale begins to wilt. Taste and adjust the seasonings as desired. Serve hot.

VARIATIONS

- For a spicier dish, sprinkle in chili powder or crushed red pepper flakes to taste as the mixture cooks.
- Replace the kale with any other dark leafy greens of your choice.

Hash is typically a mixture of eggs, potatoes, and chopped bits of meat all cooked together. This vegan version is made with a colorful assortment of vegetables and seasoned tofu. Serve it with slices of whole grain toast or an English muffin for an old-fashioned diner-style breakfast.

Tofu and Vegetable hash

YIELD: 2 TO 3 SERVINGS

8 ounces firm or extra-firm regular tofu

1 teaspoon tamari

1 teaspoon curry powder

¼ teaspoon dried dill weed

2 medium red-skinned potatoes, quartered lengthwise and sliced

2 teaspoons olive oil

½ cup diced green bell peppers

⅓ cup diced red onions

1½ teaspoons minced garlic

⅓ cup frozen peas

1 plum tomato, finely diced

1 tablespoon chopped fresh parsley

1 tablespoon nutritional yeast flakes

¼ teaspoon sea salt

⅛ teaspoon freshly ground black pepper

Crumble the tofu into a small bowl using your fingers. Add the tamari, curry powder, and dill weed and stir well to evenly coat the tofu. Set aside.

Place the potatoes and olive oil in a large skillet and cook over medium heat, stirring often, for 5 to 7 minutes or until lightly browned around the edges. Add the bell peppers, red onions, and garlic and cook and stir for 2 minutes.

Add the seasoned tofu and peas and cook and stir for 3 to 5 minutes or until the potatoes are fork-tender. Add the tomato, parsley, nutritional yeast flakes, salt, and pepper and cook and stir for 1 to 2 minutes or until the tomatoes are fork-tender. Taste and adjust the seasonings as desired. Serve hot.

VARIATION

Add any leftover ingredients that you have on hand to the mixture as it cooks.

Tasty Toppers

dips, dressings, and sauces

Some people like their foods simply prepared, and for them, a squeeze of lemon and maybe a light sprinkling of salt and pepper are all that is needed to enhance a dish. But most of us enjoy a little pizzazz in our meals or a special sauce to top off our creations. So whether you like to use just a dab or slather it on, this section has you covered with recipes that will tantalize your taste buds. In no time you can make creamy, dairy-free dips, dressings, sauces, or gravies to dunk your vegetables into, drizzle over your salad, or top off side dishes. Many of these recipes can also be used as condiments and spreads for breads or sandwiches or used as dips alongside your favorite crackers or chips.

Tahini and flaxseed oil give this dressing a creamy consistency, but the lemon juice, apple cider vinegar, and fresh garlic are what's responsible for its wonderful zesty flavor. It's an excellent dressing for tossed salads and slaws or for use as a sauce on steamed or cooked vegetables, grains, or pasta. After it has chilled it will thicken; it can then be used as a dip for raw vegetables, tortilla chips, or crackers.

Garlic-Tahini **dressing**

YIELD: 1½ CUPS

⅔ cup filtered water

⅓ cup tahini

¼ cup flaxseed oil or olive oil

2 tablespoons apple cider vinegar

2 tablespoons freshly squeezed lemon juice

2 tablespoons tamari

2 tablespoons minced garlic

2 tablespoons chopped fresh parsley

¼ teaspoon freshly ground black pepper

Place all of the ingredients in a blender or food processor and process for 1 to 2 minutes or until completely smooth. Use immediately or chill in the refrigerator to thicken. Stored in an airtight container in the refrigerator, Garlic-Tahini Dressing will keep for 5 to 7 days.

This creamy, dairy-free ranch dressing is made with tofu and many of the same flavorings as its dairy-based cousin. Use it as a dressing on tossed salads or slaws, a sauce for pasta or grain dishes, a spread on sandwiches, or a dip for vegetables, crackers, or chips. It can even be used as a mayonnaise replacement in your favorite recipes.

dairy-free Ranch Dressing or Dip

YIELD: 2 CUPS

8 ounces firm or extra-firm regular tofu

⅔ cup filtered water

⅓ cup olive oil

¼ cup thinly sliced green onions

4 teaspoons freshly squeezed lemon juice

1 tablespoon tamari

1 tablespoon chopped fresh parsley

1 tablespoon chopped fresh dill weed

2 teaspoons minced garlic

¼ teaspoon sea salt

⅛ teaspoon freshly ground black pepper

Pinch of cayenne

Crumble the tofu into a blender or food processor using your fingers. Add all of the remaining ingredients and process for 1 to 2 minutes or until completely smooth. Scrape down sides of the container and process an additional 30 seconds. Use immediately or chill in the refrigerator to thicken. Stored in an airtight container in the refrigerator, Dairy-Free Ranch Dressing or Dip will keep for 5 to 7 days.

Pesto means "pounded" in Italian, in reference to the mortar and pestle that is commonly used to prepare it. This all-raw pesto contains many of the traditional pesto components, plus walnuts, fresh parsley, and hemp seed oil for added flavor. Use a little or a lot, as desired, to add flavor to soups, salads, salad dressings, sauces, pasta, grains, or main dishes. It's also terrific when used as a dip or spread for vegetables, sandwiches, or slices of bread.

Herb-Walnut **pesto**

YIELD: 1 CUP

¾ cup fresh basil leaves, packed

¾ cup fresh parsley, packed

¼ cup filtered water

¼ cup chopped walnuts

2 tablespoons minced garlic

2 tablespoons hemp seed oil

2 tablespoons olive oil or flaxseed oil

¼ teaspoon sea salt

¼ teaspoon freshly ground black pepper

Place all of the ingredients in a food processor and process for 1 to 2 minutes or until the mixture forms a completely smooth paste. Serve immediately or thoroughly chilled. Stored in an airtight container, Herb-Walnut Pesto will keep for 5 to 7 days in the refrigerator or for 3 months in the freezer.

This spicy and flavorful combination is more than just mashed avocado, and it can be made as hot as you like or can handle. Serve it as a condiment or spread for sandwiches or wraps, as a topping on cooked beans or main dishes, or as a snack with tortilla chips and salsa.

chunky Guacamole

YIELD: 2 SERVINGS

1 Hass avocado, diced (about 1 cup)

2 teaspoons freshly squeezed lime juice

1 plum tomato, finely diced

1 green onion, thinly sliced

½ medium jalapeño chile, seeded and finely diced

1 teaspoon minced garlic

Hot sauce or crushed red pepper flakes

Sea salt

Freshly ground black pepper

Place the avocado and lime juice in a small glass or ceramic bowl. Using a potato masher or fork, mash the avocado until it is completely smooth. Stir in the tomato, green onion, chile, and garlic. Season with hot sauce, salt, and pepper to taste. Serve immediately or thoroughly chilled. Stored in an airtight container in the refrigerator, Chunky Guacamole will keep for 2 to 3 days.

TIP: Placing the avocado pit in the guacamole after it is prepared will help keep it from darkening and discoloring, which naturally happens when avocado is exposed to air. This is especially helpful if the guacamole will be stored or chilled before serving.

This classic salsa recipe is made with all fresh ingredients and requires only a little chopping and mixing. Serve it as a snack with tortilla chips, put it on or in your favorite tacos or burritos, or include it as part of a salad or sandwich filling.

pico de Gallo

1 cup diced plum tomatoes

⅓ cup diced red or yellow onions

⅓ cup diced green bell peppers

¼ cup thinly sliced green onions

¼ cup chopped fresh cilantro

½ medium jalapeño chile, seeded and finely diced

2 teaspoons freshly squeezed lemon or lime juice

2 teaspoons minced garlic

Sea salt

Freshly ground black pepper

Place the tomatoes, onions, bell peppers, green onions, cilantro, chile, lemon juice, and garlic in a small bowl and stir until well combined. Season with salt and pepper to taste. Serve immediately or thoroughly chilled. Stored in an airtight container in the refrigerator, Pico de Gallo will keep for 5 to 7 days.

VARIATIONS

Substitute other types of tomatoes, such as cherry, yellow, or heirloom varieties, or, in a pinch, use one can (14 ounces) diced or crushed tomatoes instead of fresh tomatoes.

Mildly flavored black beans are an excellent source of animal-free protein, and their dark color beautifully complements the delicate sweetness of fresh, golden mango and the other ingredients in this colorful salsa. Enjoy it as a snack with tortilla chips or add it to your favorite tacos or burritos. You can also combine it with grains like rice or quinoa and serve it as a salad on mixed greens, a filling for tortillas, or a stuffing for pita halves.

Black Bean and Mango salsa

YIELD: 2 CUPS

1 cup cooked black beans

1 medium mango, diced (about ½ cup)

⅓ cup diced red bell peppers

⅓ cup diced green bell peppers

¼ cup thinly sliced green onions

¼ cup chopped fresh cilantro

½ medium jalapeño chile, seeded and finely diced

1 tablespoon olive oil

2 teaspoons freshly squeezed lime juice

2 teaspoons apple cider vinegar

2 teaspoons minced garlic

2 teaspoons minced fresh ginger

¾ teaspoon dried oregano

¾ teaspoon chili powder

½ teaspoon ground cumin

¼ teaspoon sea salt

⅛ teaspoon freshly ground black pepper

Place all of the ingredients in a small bowl and stir until well combined. Serve immediately or thoroughly chilled. Stored in an airtight container in the refrigerator, Black Bean and Mango Salsa will keep for 5 to 7 days.

This nutritious variation of refried beans is referred to as "unfried" because it has no added fat. With little effort, you can add some kick to a humble can of pinto beans by incorporating jalapeño chile, garlic, and spices. Use the mixture as a spread or filling for tacos, tostadas, burritos, or sandwiches. You can also enjoy it as a dip with tortilla chips and salsa.

unfried Beans

YIELD: 2 CUPS

1 can (15 ounces) **pinto beans, drained and rinsed**

1 medium jalapeño chile, seeded and finely diced

2 tablespoons filtered water

1 tablespoon freshly squeezed lime juice

1 tablespoon minced garlic

1 teaspoon chili powder

1 teaspoon ground cumin

1 teaspoon dried oregano

½ teaspoon sea salt

¼ teaspoon freshly ground black pepper

Place all of the ingredients in a medium bowl. Using a potato masher or fork, mash the mixture until it is as smooth or chunky as you like. Serve immediately or thoroughly chilled. Stored in an airtight container, Unfried Beans will keep for 5 to 7 days in the refrigerator or for 3 months in the freezer.

VARIATIONS

Replace the pinto beans with other types of canned beans, such as black, kidney, navy, red, or even black-eyed peas.

TIPS:

- For a very smooth spread, place all of the ingredients in a food processor and process for 1 to 2 minutes or until completely smooth.
- For a milder spread, simply omit the jalapeño chile.

The traditional flavors of Middle Eastern hummus are transformed by adding a few chopped olives and a little toasted sesame oil and balsamic vinegar. Serve it alongside cut pita bread, crackers, or assorted raw vegetables as a snack, or use it as a filling for sandwiches or wraps.

Olive hummus

YIELD: 2 CUPS

½ cup pitted olives of choice

1 can (15 ounces) chickpeas, drained and rinsed

3 large cloves garlic

2 tablespoons filtered water

2 tablespoons freshly squeezed lemon juice

2 tablespoons balsamic vinegar

1 tablespoon toasted sesame oil

1 tablespoon tahini

½ teaspoon ground cumin

¼ teaspoon sea salt

⅛ teaspoon freshly ground black pepper

Place the olives in a food processor and pulse several times until coarsely chopped. Remove ¼ cup of the chopped olives and set aside. Add all of the remaining ingredients to the food processor and process for 1 to 2 minutes or until completely smooth. Scrape down the sides of the container and process for 30 seconds longer.

Transfer the hummus to a medium bowl and stir in the reserved chopped olives. Serve immediately or thoroughly chilled. Stored in an airtight container, Olive Hummus will keep for 5 to 7 days in the refrigerator or for 3 months in the freezer.

VARIATIONS

For a spicy flavor, omit the olives and balsamic vinegar and add other seasonings, like curry powder or chili powder, prior to blending.

Nutritional yeast flakes, which have a remarkable cheeselike flavor, are showcased in this versatile vegan version of cheese sauce. Just two tablespoons of these delicious flakes go a long way when it comes to boosting the nutritional value of foods and adding supplemental vitamin B$_{12}$ to your diet. Use this sauce as a topping for baked potatoes, french fries, steamed vegetables, grains, or pasta, or to enhance the flavor and texture of soups and stews.

special "Cheese" Sauce

YIELD: 1½ CUPS

½ cup nutritional yeast flakes

¼ cup whole wheat pastry flour

½ teaspoon chili powder

½ teaspoon garlic powder

½ teaspoon sea salt

1½ cups soymilk or other nondairy milk of choice

1 tablespoon safflower oil

1 teaspoon Dijon mustard

Place the nutritional yeast flakes, flour, chili powder, garlic powder, and salt in a small saucepan and whisk them together. Whisk in the soymilk, safflower oil, and mustard. Place over low heat and cook, stirring often, for 3 to 5 minutes or until thickened. Serve hot. Stored in an airtight container in the refrigerator, Special "Cheese" Sauce will keep for 5 to 7 days.

Homemade vegan gravy is very easy to make and only takes a few minutes, so you'll never have to go without gravy again at another family get-together or holiday meal. Serve it on top of your favorite vegetables, mashed potatoes, biscuits, grains, or main dishes. It can also be used as a sauce for casseroles or be added to soups or stews.

golden Gravy

YIELD: 2 CUPS

⅓ cup finely diced yellow onions

1½ teaspoons olive oil

2 teaspoons minced garlic

2 cups vegetable broth or filtered water

⅓ cup nutritional yeast flakes

¼ cup whole wheat pastry flour

4 teaspoons tamari

1 teaspoon dried thyme

½ teaspoon sea salt

⅛ teaspoon freshly ground black pepper

Place the onions and olive oil in a small saucepan and cook over low heat, stirring often, for 2 to 3 minutes or until soft. Add the garlic and cook and stir for 1 minute.

Place all of the remaining ingredients in a small bowl and whisk them together until completely smooth and free of lumps. Whisk this mixture into the onions mixture and cook, stirring often, for 2 to 3 minutes or until thickened. Taste and adjust the seasonings as desired. Serve hot. Stored in an airtight container in the refrigerator, leftover Golden Gravy will keep for 5 to 7 days.

TIP: This gravy can be made in larger batches, cooled completely, portioned into airtight containers, and frozen for up to 3 months. Simply thaw the portions needed and reheat them before using.

Super Soups and Salads

Sure, you could just hit your neighborhood salad bar or fill your stomach easily by simply opening a can of soup, but making soup and salad yourself gives you total control over the ingredients and flavors they contain. All too often, eateries and manufacturers use excessive amounts of salt and fat to over-compensate for the lack of flavor and nourishment in their products. You'll be amazed at how easy it is to cook up a pot of your own homemade soup or chili or toss a salad made with lots of fresh, crunchy ingredients instead of bland iceberg lettuce and a wedge of tomato. This chapter also features raw vegetable and pasta combinations, a mixed bean salad, and even a tofu-based mock chicken salad. Prepare one of these selections whenever you need a light lunch or supper, or combine a few to create a filling evening meal.

This miso-based soup, made with tofu, mushrooms, and Swiss chard, has a rich and earthy flavor. It's so quick and easy to make that you can be enjoying a bowlful in under ten minutes. Pair it with a salad of mixed greens and a handful of crackers or a slice of bread for a light yet filling meal.

Miso soup

YIELD: 3 TO 4 SERVINGS

4 ounces firm or extra-firm regular tofu, diced

2 teaspoons olive oil

1 cup thinly sliced shiitake mushrooms

½ cup thinly sliced green onions

1 tablespoon minced garlic

1 tablespoon minced fresh ginger

4 cups filtered water or vegetable broth

2 leaves Swiss chard or other greens of choice, stemmed and chopped (about 1½ cups)

2 tablespoons miso of choice

1½ teaspoons toasted sesame oil

2 teaspoons sesame seeds

Place the tofu and olive oil in a medium saucepan and cook over medium heat for 2 minutes, stirring often. Add the mushrooms, green onions, garlic, and ginger and cook and stir for 2 minutes. Add the water and Swiss chard and bring to a boil over high heat. Lower the heat and simmer for 3 minutes. Remove from the heat.

Stir together the miso and a few tablespoons of the soup broth. Add the miso mixture, toasted sesame oil, and sesame seeds to the soup and stir until well combined. Serve hot.

VARIATIONS

- Add or substitute other varieties of fresh or dried mushrooms or vegetables.
- Add cooked pasta or grains to the soup shortly before serving.

This soup's golden broth is surprisingly similar to chicken soup in both flavor and appearance, but of course it is totally animal free. This trick is achieved by using a combination of dried herbs, seasonings, and nutritional yeast flakes, and by blending some of the cooked vegetables.

golden vegetable Noodle Soup

YIELD: 3 TO 4 SERVINGS

1 cup diced yellow onions

1 cup diced carrots

1 cup diced celery

2 teaspoons olive oil

4 teaspoons minced garlic

5 cups filtered water or vegetable broth

1 bay leaf

1 teaspoon sea salt

½ teaspoon dried thyme

¼ teaspoon freshly ground black pepper

½ cup whole grain rotini or other small pasta of choice

⅓ cup chopped fresh parsley

2 tablespoons nutritional yeast flakes

½ teaspoon dried dill weed

⅛ teaspoon turmeric or curry powder

Place the onions, carrots, celery, and olive oil in a large saucepan or pot and cook over medium heat, stirring often, for 2 to 3 minutes to soften. Add the garlic and cook and stir for 1 minute. Stir in 4 cups of the water and the bay leaf, salt, thyme, and pepper and bring to a boil over high heat. Cover, reduce the heat to low, and simmer for 10 minutes.

Transfer 1 cup of the soup to a blender or food processor. Add the remaining 1 cup water and process for 1 minute or until completely smooth. Stir the blended mixture into the saucepan along with the rotini, parsley, nutritional yeast flakes, dill weed, and turmeric and simmer for 8 to 10 minutes or until the rotini is tender. Taste and adjust the seasonings as desired.

VARIATION

Omit the pasta and add a small amount (about ½ to ¾ cup) of leftover cooked rice or grains.

This fat-free carrot soup is a snap to make and so delicious. Carrots are rich in beta-carotene (vitamin A) and vitamins B, C, and E, so this is a great soup to make when you are under the weather or feel a cold coming on.

Ginger-Carrot soup

YIELD: 3 TO 4 SERVINGS

1 pound carrots, sliced (about 4 to 5 cups)

3 cups filtered water or vegetable broth

¾ cup diced yellow onions

½ cup freshly squeezed orange juice

1 tablespoon minced fresh ginger

1 tablespoon minced garlic

½ teaspoon sea salt

¼ teaspoon ground cinnamon

Place all of the ingredients in a large saucepan or pot and bring to a boil over high heat. Cover, reduce the heat to low, and simmer for 10 to 15 minutes or until the carrots are tender.

Remove from the heat and let cool for 10 minutes. Carefully transfer the mixture to a blender or food processor and process until completely smooth. Return the soup to the saucepan. Taste and adjust the seasonings as desired. Serve hot.

VARIATIONS

- For a spicy flavor, add a little curry powder to taste.
- For a creamier consistency, add a few tablespoons of soymilk or nut butter.

When hunger hits, there is nothing like a big bowl of bean soup and a slice of bread for a simple and satisfying meal. Some cooks can't image making bean soup without a ham hock or slab or two of bacon, but this hearty, meatless bean soup shows just how easy and deliciously it can be done, so we can all proudly say, "Let the piggy live and run." Use any kind of canned beans you have on hand or most prefer. Try navy beans, pinto beans, red beans, black beans, mixed beans, or even lentils—whichever one suits your mood and taste buds.

bean bag Soup

YIELD: 3 TO 4 SERVINGS

¾ cup diced yellow onions

¾ cup diced carrots

¾ cup diced celery

1½ teaspoons olive oil

1 tablespoon minced garlic

4 cups filtered water

1 can (15 ounces) beans of choice, drained and rinsed

1 tablespoon tamari

1 teaspoon dried basil

1 teaspoon dried oregano

½ teaspoon dried thyme

½ teaspoon sea salt

¼ teaspoon freshly ground black pepper

Place the onions, carrots, celery, and olive oil in a large saucepan or pot and cook over medium heat, stirring often, for 2 to 3 minutes to soften. Add the garlic and cook and stir for 1 minute. Stir in all of the remaining ingredients and cook for 10 minutes or until the vegetables are tender. Taste and adjust the seasonings as desired. Serve hot.

VARIATIONS

For variety or to add more bulk to the soup, add chopped greens, potatoes, or leftover vegetables or pasta.

This colorful chili is soy free, packed with vegetables and several kinds of beans, and quite filling. Eat it by the bowlful, use it as a topping for a baked potato or garnet yam, or combine it with grains for a hearty entrée or as part of a filling for wraps. You can also enjoy it either hot or cold as a chunky dip with tortilla chips or crackers.

Vegetable Patch chili

YIELD: 3 TO 4 SERVINGS

⅔ cup diced red onions

⅔ cup diced carrots

⅔ cup diced celery

⅔ cup diced zucchinis

⅔ cup fresh or frozen corn kernels

⅔ cup diced green or red bell peppers

1 medium jalapeño chile, seeded and finely diced

1 tablespoon minced garlic

1 tablespoon olive oil

1 can (14 ounces) **crushed tomatoes**

1 can (14 ounces) **diced tomatoes**

1 can (15 ounces) **mixed beans, drained and rinsed**

1 tablespoon chili powder

1 teaspoon ground cumin

1 teaspoon dried oregano

½ teaspoon sea salt

¼ teaspoon freshly ground black pepper

¼ cup chopped fresh cilantro or parsley

Place the onions, carrots, celery, zucchinis, corn, bell peppers, chile, garlic, and olive oil in a large saucepan or pot and cook over medium heat, stirring often, for 5 to 7 minutes or until the vegetables are fork-tender. Add the crushed and diced tomatoes, beans, chili powder, cumin, oregano, salt, and pepper and stir until well combined. Cover, reduce the heat to low, and simmer for 10 minutes. Stir in the cilantro. Taste and adjust the seasonings as desired. Serve hot.

TIP: Vary the flavor and heat of this chili to suit your own personal tastes. If you like it mild, cut back on the chili powder; for a little extra kick, add more. If you're in a particularly spicy mood or like it really hot, add a little cayenne or hot sauce.

This is not your typical deli-style coleslaw by any means. This crunchy vegetable slaw features a dazzling blend of vibrant colors and textures and a tangy, Dijon mustard vinaigrette. Servings of the slaw can be rolled up in a tortilla for a quick wrap, or try topping it with grains or pasta for a hearty one-plate meal.

colorful Coleslaw

YIELD: 2 TO 3 SERVINGS

SALAD

2 leaves purple kale, stemmed and chopped (about 1½ cups)

2 leaves collard greens, stemmed and chopped (about 1½ cups)

½ cup shredded green cabbage

½ cup shredded red cabbage

½ cup shredded carrots

½ cup peeled and shredded gold beets

1 celery stalk, diced

1 green onion, thinly sliced

¼ cup chopped fresh parsley

DRESSING

1 tablespoon olive oil

1 tablespoon apple cider vinegar

1 tablespoon Dijon mustard

1 tablespoon agave nectar

¼ teaspoon sea salt

¼ teaspoon freshly ground black pepper

To make the salad, place the kale, collard greens, and green and red cabbage in a medium bowl and toss them together. Add all of the remaining vegetables and toss again.

To make the dressing, place all of the ingredients in a small bowl and whisk them together. Drizzle the dressing over the slaw and toss until the vegetables are evenly coated. Alternatively, drizzle the dressing over individual servings as desired. Serve immediately.

VARIATION

For a creamy coleslaw, add a few tablespoons of vegan mayonnaise to the dressing.

This large salad, made with plenty of fresh vegetables and greens, is eye-catching and sure to satisfy any appetite. You can turn this salad into a vegetable-packed sandwich by stuffing it into pita bread or wrapping it in tortillas.

A Gigantic Garden salad bowl

YIELD: 2 SERVINGS

3 cups mixed baby greens or chopped lettuce of choice (see tip)

¾ cup small broccoli florets

¾ cup small cauliflower florets

½ cup shredded purple cabbage

½ cup shredded carrots

½ cup thinly sliced cucumbers

½ cup thinly sliced radishes

1 celery stalk, diced

4 cherry tomatoes, halved

½ cup canned chickpeas or other beans of choice, drained and rinsed

2 tablespoons raw sunflower seeds

2 tablespoons raw pumpkin seeds or hemp seeds

Salad dressing of choice

Place the mixed greens and all of the cut vegetables in a large bowl, either decoratively in layers or rows or simply tossed together. Sprinkle the beans and seeds over the top. Drizzle salad dressing to taste over the entire salad and toss until all of the ingredients are evenly coated. Alternatively, drizzle the dressing over individual servings as desired. Serve immediately.

TIP: For ease and convenience, use prewashed, bagged baby greens (also known as mesclun) or lettuce.

A variety of beans adds extra color, while crunchy fresh vegetables lend texture to this flavorful combo. Serve it as a side dish or a one-plate meal, combined with pasta or grains on mixed greens, if you like. Or enjoy it as a sandwich filling with lettuce and other vegetables stuffed in pita bread or wrapped in tortillas.

calico Bean Salad

YIELD: 2½ CUPS (3 TO 5 SERVINGS)

1 can (15 ounces) **mixed beans, drained and rinsed**

1 plum tomato, finely diced

1 celery stalk, finely diced

3 tablespoons finely diced red onions

1 green onion, thinly sliced

2 tablespoons chopped fresh parsley

1 tablespoon olive oil

1 tablespoon apple cider vinegar or red wine vinegar

1 teaspoon ground cumin

½ teaspoon chili powder

¼ teaspoon sea salt

⅛ teaspoon freshly ground black pepper

Place all of the ingredients in a medium bowl and stir until well combined. Set aside for several minutes before serving to allow the flavors to blend.

TIP: Many companies sell cans of mixed beans, but you can use any variety of beans in this salad that you most prefer or have on hand.

Versatile tofu does double duty as both a base and dressing ingredient in this recipe. A creamy dressing is created by blending tofu with other ingredients and then combining it with pieces of seasoned, baked tofu, chopped celery, and green onions. The end result is a tofu-based salad reminiscent of chicken salad, but with only a fraction of the fat and no cholesterol. Enjoy it as a side dish or serve it on mixed greens for a heartier meal. It also makes a tasty filling for sandwiches, pita bread, or tortillas—just add lettuce leaves and tomato slices.

unchicken Tofu Salad

YIELD: 3 CUPS (4 TO 6 SERVINGS)

SALAD

2 cups Seasoned Tofu Tidbits (page 74), cooled

1 celery stalk, diced

1 green onion, thinly sliced

2 tablespoons chopped fresh parsley

DRESSING

¼ cup firm or extra-firm regular tofu

2 tablespoons filtered water

2 tablespoons olive oil

4 teaspoons Dijon mustard

4 teaspoons maple syrup

1 tablespoon apple cider vinegar

1 teaspoon celery seeds

½ teaspoon garlic powder

½ teaspoon onion powder

¼ teaspoon sea salt

¼ teaspoon freshly ground black pepper

To make the salad, place all of the salad ingredients in a medium bowl and stir them together.

To make the dressing, crumble the tofu into a blender or food processor using your fingers. Add all of the remaining dressing ingredients and process for 1 to 2 minutes or until completely smooth. Scrape down the sides of the container and process for 30 seconds longer. Pour the dressing over the tofu salad and stir until well combined. Serve immediately or thoroughly chilled.

TIP: The salad will thicken when chilled.

You don't always have to cook up a pot of noodles when you get a hankering for pasta salad. This recipe doesn't contain any pasta at all; instead, a vegetable peeler is ingeniously used to make long thin strips of fettuccine-shaped "noodles" out of carrots, yellow squash, and zucchini. The flavors and textures of this colorful raw salad will make your taste buds come alive.

Raw Pasta **primavera**

YIELD: 2 SERVINGS

2 medium carrots

1 medium yellow squash

1 medium zucchini

⅔ cup diced red or orange bell peppers

1 green onion, thinly sliced

2 tablespoons chopped fresh basil

2 tablespoons chopped fresh parsley

4 teaspoons olive oil

1 tablespoon freshly squeezed lemon juice

1 tablespoon raw hemp seeds or sesame seeds

2 teaspoons minced garlic

Sea salt

Freshly ground black pepper

Crushed red pepper flakes

To make the vegetables noodles, leave the carrots whole and slice the yellow squash and zucchini in half lengthwise. Make a V-shaped cut to remove most of the seed section from the yellow squash and zucchini, and slice the removed seed section into long, thin strips. Use a vegetable peeler to shave long strips down the entire length of each of the carrots and the yellow squash and zucchini halves.

Place the vegetable noodles in a medium bowl. Add all of the remaining ingredients and season with salt, pepper, and crushed red pepper flakes to taste. Gently toss until the vegetables are evenly coated. Taste and adjust the seasonings as desired. Gently toss the mixture again. Serve immediately.

Cooked pasta and a colorful assortment of fresh vegetables comprise the base of this salad, but it's the vinaigrette that they're tossed in that steals the show. It has a sweet-and-spicy flavor that will have you coming back for more, and it is definitely a crowd pleaser at any picnic. It can be served as is or on mixed greens, if you like.

Maple-Mustard **pasta salad**

YIELD: 2 TO 3 SERVINGS

SALAD

6 ounces small whole grain pasta of choice (such as elbow macaroni or penne)

¾ cup small broccoli florets

⅓ cup finely diced carrots

⅓ cup finely diced red bell peppers

⅓ cup finely diced zucchini

⅓ cup finely diced yellow squash

⅓ cup thinly sliced green onions

DRESSING

3 tablespoons olive oil

3 tablespoons red wine vinegar

4 teaspoons maple syrup

4 teaspoons Dijon or whole grain mustard

¾ teaspoon dried basil

¾ teaspoon dried oregano

¾ teaspoon sea salt

½ teaspoon freshly ground black pepper

To cook the pasta, fill a large saucepan two-thirds full with filtered water and bring to a boil over medium-high heat. Add the pasta and cook, stirring occasionally, according to the time on the package instructions or until tender.

Drain the pasta in a colander, rinse it with cold water, and drain it well again. Transfer the pasta to a medium bowl and add all of the salad vegetables. Gently toss until well combined.

To make the dressing, place all of the ingredients in a small bowl and whisk until well combined. Pour the dressing over the salad and gently toss until the pasta and vegetables are evenly coated. Cover with plastic wrap and refrigerate for 30 minutes or longer before serving to allow the flavors to blend.

VARIATIONS

- For more visual appeal, try spinach-flavored or tricolored pasta.
- Add or substitute other cut vegetables that you prefer or have on hand.

From Hand to Mouth

sandwiches and wraps

We all love eating with our fingers, and nothing compares to wrapping our hands around a hearty sandwich. Hand-friendly wraps are extremely popular because they easily hold a variety of ingredients. As a result, wraps have started to make an appearance at lunch, dinner, and even breakfast. For handy eating, this section has all of your meals fully covered. In the morning, try a simple tortilla filled with fruit and nut butter or wrapped around leftovers. Fulfill your lunch or dinner needs with a shredded vegetable-and-spread wrap or grab a hefty burrito. When you're yearning for something really impressive, try one of the hot or cold deli-style sandwich selections.

Here's a new spin on the classic peanut butter and jelly sandwich, made a bit more substantial with the addition of sliced bananas, raisins, and sunflower seeds. Enjoy this wrap for breakfast or lunch or as a snack.

Nana Nutter roll-ups

YIELD: 2 WRAPS

2 (8-inch) **flour tortillas**

2 to 4 tablespoons **unsalted smooth or crunchy peanut butter or other nut butter of choice**

2 to 4 tablespoons **fruit jelly or jam of choice**

1 to 2 teaspoons **raisins**

1 to 2 teaspoons **raw sunflower seeds**

1 medium **banana, thinly sliced**

For easier rolling, warm each tortilla in a large skillet over medium heat for 1 to 2 minutes per side, or warm in a microwave oven for 20 to 30 seconds.

To assemble each roll-up, place a tortilla flat on a large cutting board or work surface. Spread 1 to 2 tablespoons of the nut butter in a horizontal line in the center of the tortilla. Top the nut butter with 1 to 2 tablespoons of the jelly. Sprinkle with half of the raisins and sunflower seeds. Place half of the banana slices on top.

To roll each roll-up, fold the bottom half of the tortilla over the filling ingredients, fold the sides of the tortilla toward the center, and then roll up the tortilla from the bottom edge to enclose the filling.

Fill and assemble the remaining tortilla in the same fashion. Serve the roll-ups immediately, or wrap them tightly in plastic wrap or place them in an airtight container. Stored in the refrigerator, Nana Nutter Roll-Ups will keep for 1 to 2 days.

VARIATIONS

- Replace the fruit jelly with a light drizzle of agave nectar or maple syrup.
- Replace the banana with slices of other fresh fruit or berries.
- Omit the tortillas and assemble the ingredients on toasted slices of bread, split bagels, or English muffins.

More of us are reaching for something to grab and go for eating on the run, especially when we're short on time or running late. This led to the cunning invention of the popular breakfast burrito: typical breakfast fare favorites rolled up in a tortilla for easy portability. This burrito, filled with leftover Tofu and Vegetable Hash plus a few other ingredients, is perfect for munching on for breakfast or any other time of the day.

brunch and munch Burritos

YIELD: 2 BURRITOS

2 (8-inch) **flour tortillas**

2 cups **Tofu and Vegetable Hash** (page 37)

2 slices **vegan cheese of choice**, or ½ cup shredded vegan cheese of choice

1 **plum tomato, thinly sliced**

For easier rolling, warm each tortilla in a large skillet over medium heat for 1 to 2 minutes per side, or warm in a microwave oven for 20 to 30 seconds.

To assemble each burrito, place a tortilla flat on a large cutting board or work surface. Spoon half of the Tofu and Vegetable Hash in a horizontal line in the center of the tortilla. Top with one slice of the vegan cheese and half of the tomato slices.

To roll each burrito, fold the bottom half of the tortilla over the filling ingredients, fold the sides of the tortilla toward the center, and then roll up the tortilla from the bottom edge to enclose the filling.

Fill and assemble the remaining tortilla in the same fashion. Serve the burritos immediately, or wrap them tightly in plastic wrap or place them in an airtight container. Stored in the refrigerator, Brunch and Munch Burritos will keep for 2 to 3 days.

"SAUSAGE" AND HOME FRIES BURRITOS

Replace the Tofu and Vegetable Hash, vegan cheese, and tomato with 1 cup leftover Hacienda Home-Fries (page 35) and 1 cup crumbled Sweet Italian "Sausages" (page 34).

These all-raw wraps, made from fresh lettuce leaves filled with a chopped salad mixture and light dressing, are rolled and eaten like burritos, their tortilla-based cousins.

crunchy Lettuce Wraps

YIELD: 4 WRAPS (2 SERVINGS)

5 leaves red-tipped leaf lettuce or other lettuce of choice

1 plum tomato, finely diced

½ cup finely diced celery

½ cup finely diced cucumbers

½ cup finely diced red or orange bell peppers

¼ cup thinly sliced green onions

¼ cup chopped fresh cilantro or parsley

¼ cup raw pumpkin seeds

Olive oil

Freshly squeezed lemon juice or vinegar of choice

Sea salt

Freshly ground black pepper

S et aside 4 of the lettuce leaves. Coarsely chop the remaining lettuce leaf and place it in a medium bowl. Stir in the tomato, celery, cucumbers, bell peppers, green onions, cilantro, and pumpkin seeds. Drizzle a little olive oil and lemon juice to taste over the vegetables and season with salt and pepper to taste. Gently toss until well combined.

To assemble the lettuce wraps, place the reserved 4 lettuce leaves vertically on a large cutting board or work surface. Place equal spoonfuls of the vegetable filling mixture near the stem end of each of the leaves.

Fold the sides of each leaf toward the center. Starting at the stem end, roll up the length of the leaf to enclose the filling. End with the seam side down. Repeat the rolling procedure for the remaining lettuce leaves.

Serve immediately, or wrap them tightly in plastic wrap or place them in an airtight container. Stored in the refrigerator, Crunchy Lettuce Wraps will keep for 1 to 2 days.

These tortilla wraps are rolled to resemble small, vegetable-filled cornucopias. They are made with your choice of spread, with layers of fresh vegetables bursting out of their open tops. Enjoy one for lunch or as a snack. You can also make a large tray containing several varieties with assorted spreads and vegetable fillings and serve them at a party.

vibrant Vegetable Cornucopias

YIELD: 2 WRAPS

2 (8-inch) **flour tortillas**

Spread or condiment of choice (see tip)

2 leaves leaf lettuce or other lettuce of choice

½ cup shredded carrots

½ cup shredded zucchinis

1 plum tomato, thinly sliced

½ cup thinly sliced cucumber

½ cup alfalfa sprouts or other fresh sprouts of choice

For easier rolling, warm each tortilla in a large skillet over medium heat for 1 to 2 minutes per side, or warm in a microwave oven for 20 to 30 seconds.

To assemble each wrap, place a tortilla flat on a large cutting board or work surface. Apply the spread or condiment over the top half of the tortilla, leaving a 1-inch border around the edges. Place 1 lettuce leaf vertically in the center of the tortilla so that it hangs over top edge slightly. Layer half of each shredded vegetable, half of the tomato slices, half of the cucumber slices, and half of the sprouts on top of the lettuce.

To create the cornucopia, fold the bottom of the tortilla up to the center, and then fold in each side, one overlapping the other to enclose the vegetables. Secure the wrap with a toothpick, threading it through both sides.

Assemble and roll the remaining tortilla in the same fashion. Serve immediately, or wrap them tightly in plastic wrap or place them in an airtight container. Stored in the refrigerator, Vibrant Vegetable Cornucopias will keep for 2 to 3 days.

VARIATION

Replace any of the suggested vegetables with other fresh vegetables to suit your tastes.

TIP: For the spread or condiment, use mustard, vegan mayonnaise, hummus, or your favorite mashed bean spread.

Falafels are chickpea-based patties or balls that are cooked or deep-fried in hot oil. They are commonly served in most Middle Eastern homes and restaurants and at roadside stands. These falafels are tinted and flavored with sun-dried tomatoes and a generous dose of spices. They're best enjoyed stuffed into pita bread as sandwiches, but they can also be eaten on their own or dipped into plain soy yogurt or tahini sauce as a snack.

sun-dried tomato Falafels in Pitas

YIELD: 2 SANDWICHES

¼ cup sun-dried tomato pieces

⅓ cup filtered water

1 cup canned chickpeas, drained and rinsed

2 teaspoons minced garlic

1½ teaspoons olive oil

1 teaspoon chili powder

1 teaspoon curry powder

¼ teaspoon sea salt

⅛ teaspoon cayenne

⅓ cup whole wheat flour

2 tablespoons finely diced red onions

2 tablespoons finely diced celery

2 tablespoons chopped fresh parsley

2 (6-inch) whole grain pita breads

Sliced cucumbers

Shredded carrots

Shredded lettuce

Alfalfa sprouts

Plain soy yogurt or tahini

Freshly squeezed lemon juice or filtered water, as needed

Place the sun-dried tomato pieces in a small bowl. Cover with the water and set aside for 5 to 10 minutes to rehydrate. Drain off any excess water and transfer the sun-dried tomato pieces to a food processor along with the chickpeas, garlic, olive oil, chili powder, curry powder, salt, and cayenne.

Process for 1 to 2 minutes or until completely smooth. Transfer the mixture to a medium bowl. Stir in the flour, onions, celery, and chopped parsley.

Pour enough olive oil into a large skillet to coat the bottom and place over medium heat. Carefully portion 6 rounded tablespoonfuls of the falafel mixture into the hot oil and flatten each one slightly with the back of the spoon. Cook the patties over medium heat for 3 to 5 minutes or until golden brown on the bottom. Flip the patties over with a metal or heatproof spatula and cook for an additional 2 to 3 minutes or until golden brown on the other side.

Place two paper towels on a large plate. Transfer the patties to the plate to allow any excess oil to drain off. Portion, cook, and drain the remaining falafel mixture in the same fashion.

To assemble each sandwich, split the pita bread in half and open the pocket of each half slightly. Fill each pita half with 3 falafel patties and as much sliced cucumbers, shredded carrots, shredded lettuce, and alfalfa sprouts as desired. Thin the soy yogurt or tahini with a small amount of lemon juice or water to make a sauce, and drizzle it over each pita half to taste.

Most deli menus include several varieties of sandwiches, including large heroes (also known as submarines, grinders, and hoagies) made with assorted ingredients layered on slices of plain or toasted bread. The fresh produce that is so abundantly available at West Coast farmers markets was the inspiration for these hero sandwiches. Crisp fresh vegetables are stacked in layers to create sandwiches that are as beautiful to behold as they are delicious to eat.

Health-Nut **heroes**

YIELD: 2 SANDWICHES

4 slices whole grain bread of choice

Dijon mustard or other condiment of choice

½ cup thinly sliced cucumbers

½ avocado, thinly sliced

1 plum tomato, thinly sliced

½ cup shredded carrots

½ cup alfalfa sprouts or other sprouts of choice

Place all of the bread slices on a large cutting board or work surface and spread them with mustard to taste. Evenly layer the vegetables, in the order listed, over two slices of the bread.

Place the remaining two slices of bread on top of the vegetables, mustard side in. Carefully slice the sandwiches in half diagonally before serving. Serve the sandwiches immediately, or wrap them tightly in plastic wrap or place them in an airtight container. Stored in the refrigerator, Health Nut Heroes will keep for 1 to 2 days.

TIPS

- Lightly toasting the bread before assembling the sandwiches will make them easier to cut.
- If you're intimidated by the stacked layers of this sandwich, give them more stability by using toothpicks to secure the layers before cutting.

These burritos are packed with flavor and fiber from the seasoned cooked vegetable mixture and the addition of a vegan cheese and crisp lettuce. They are better tasting and better for you than the bean burritos found in most Mexican restaurants, which often contain hidden animal-based ingredients.

bandito Burritos

⅓ cup diced red onions

⅓ cup fresh or frozen corn kernels

⅓ cup diced red bell peppers

1 medium jalapeño chile, seeded and finely diced

1½ teaspoons olive oil

1 cup canned pinto beans, drained and rinsed

1 plum tomato, finely diced

1 tablespoon minced garlic

½ teaspoon chili powder

½ teaspoon dried oregano

¼ teaspoon sea salt

⅛ teaspoon freshly ground black pepper

2 (8-inch) flour tortillas

½ cup shredded vegan cheese of choice

⅔ cup shredded lettuce

Place the red onions, corn, bell peppers, chile, and olive oil in a small skillet and cook over medium heat, stirring often, for 2 minutes to soften. Add the pinto beans, tomato, garlic, chili powder, oregano, salt, and pepper and cook and stir for 2 minutes. Remove from the heat.

For easier rolling, warm each tortilla in a large skillet over medium heat for 1 to 2 minutes per side, or warm in a microwave oven for 20 to 30 seconds.

To assemble each burrito, place a tortilla flat on a large cutting board or work surface. Place half of the cooked vegetable mixture in a horizontal line in the center of the tortilla. Top with half of the shredded vegan cheese and lettuce.

To roll each burrito, fold the bottom half of the tortilla over the filling ingredients, fold the sides of the tortilla toward the center, and then roll up from the bottom edge to enclose the filling.

Fill and assemble the remaining tortilla in the same fashion. Serve the burritos immediately, or wrap them tightly in plastic wrap or place them in an airtight container. Stored in the refrigerator, Bandito Burritos will keep for 2 to 3 days.

VARIATION

Add vegan sour cream, sliced avocado, or Chunky Guacamole (page 42) to taste.

Traditional submarine sandwiches are usually made with slices of deli meats and cheese, shredded lettuce, onions, and tomatoes, and are dripping with Italian dressing. Of course, a good sub doesn't have to be made with animal-based ingredients to be filling. You'll find that these cruelty-free sandwiches, made with only vegan ingredients, are just as satisfying.

Italian Sub **sandwiches**

YIELD: 2 SANDWICHES

2 (6-inch) **Italian submarine rolls or other rolls of choice**

2 leaves **romaine lettuce or other lettuce of choice**

½ cup thinly sliced **yellow or red onions**

½ cup thinly sliced **red or orange bell peppers**

½ cup thinly sliced **zucchinis**

1 plum tomato, thinly sliced (6 to 8 slices)

¼ cup thinly sliced pitted **olives of choice**

Olive oil

Red wine vinegar

Dried oregano

Freshly ground black pepper

2 slices **vegan mozzarella or other vegan cheese of choice**

Split the Italian rolls in half lengthwise and open them up. Place the rolls on a large cutting board or work surface. Layer the vegetables and olives in the order listed, dividing them evenly between the bottom halves of each roll. Drizzle a little olive oil and red wine vinegar to taste over the vegetables. Generously season the vegetables with oregano and pepper to taste.

Place a slice of the vegan cheese on top of the seasoned vegetables. Replace the top half of each roll. Carefully slice each sandwich in half before serving. Serve the sandwiches immediately, or wrap them tightly in plastic wrap or place them in an airtight container. Stored in the refrigerator, Italian Sub Sandwiches will keep for 1 to 2 days.

VARIATION

For a spicy twist, add a little mustard and/or crushed red pepper flakes.

Nowadays, you can purchase various flavors of vegan meatless meatballs; just look in the frozen food section of most supermarkets and natural food stores. Meatless meatballs only require a brief reheating and can be added to sauces, casseroles, and main dishes. Use them to quickly make these savory sandwiches, which are topped with a homemade mushroom-tomato sauce.

mushroom marinara "Meatball" Sandwiches

YIELD: 2 SANDWICHES

½ cup chopped cremini mushrooms

⅓ cup diced yellow onions

1½ teaspoons olive oil

2 teaspoons minced garlic

1 teaspoon balsamic vinegar

1 teaspoon Italian seasoning blend, or ½ teaspoon dried basil and ½ teaspoon dried oregano

½ teaspoon sea salt

¼ teaspoon freshly ground black pepper

¼ teaspoon crushed red pepper flakes

1 can (14 ounces) crushed tomatoes

8 frozen meatless meatballs (about 6 ounces)

1½ teaspoons nutritional yeast flakes

2 (6-inch) Italian submarine rolls or hot dog buns

Shredded vegan mozzarella cheese or nutritional yeast flakes

Place the mushrooms, onions, and olive oil in a small saucepan and cook over medium heat, stirring often, for 2 to 3 minutes to soften. Add the garlic, balsamic vinegar, and seasonings and cook and stir for 1 minute. Stir in the crushed tomatoes, meatless meatballs, and nutritional yeast flakes. Reduce the heat to low and simmer for 5 to 6 minutes or until the meatless meatballs are heated through. Remove from the heat.

To assemble each sandwich, partially split open the submarine roll. Spread a little of the sauce on the bottom of the split roll. Place 4 of the meatless meatballs inside the roll and top them with a little more sauce. Sprinkle vegan cheese to taste over the top. Serve hot.

Fill and assemble the other sandwich in the same fashion if you will be serving it immediately. Store any remaining sandwich ingredients separately in the refrigerator for 3 to 5 days.

SPAGHETTI AND MEATLESS MEATBALLS

For a delicious main dish for dinner, instead of making sandwiches, top cooked spaghetti or your favorite pasta with the mushroom-tomato sauce, meatless meatballs, and shredded vegan cheese or nutritional yeast flakes to taste.

In this vegan version of an American favorite, strips of seitan are cooked along with onions, mushrooms, and peppers, and topped with vegan cheese. Purchase prepackaged seitan in a block or in chunks, because you will need to thinly slice it into strips for use in this recipe.

supreme Seitan Cheesesteaks

YIELD: 2 SANDWICHES

8 ounces prepackaged seitan

½ cup thinly sliced yellow onions

½ cup halved and thinly sliced cremini mushrooms

½ cup thinly sliced green bell peppers

½ cup thinly sliced red bell peppers

1 tablespoon olive oil

1 tablespoon minced garlic

1½ teaspoons tamari

¼ teaspoon crushed red pepper flakes

Sea salt

Freshly ground black pepper

2 (6-inch) Italian submarine rolls or hot dog buns

2 slices vegan cheese of choice, or ½ cup shredded

Remove the seitan from its packaging and drain off the liquid (see tip). Lightly pat the seitan dry with a paper towel and thinly slice it into strips.

Place the onions, mushrooms, bell peppers, and olive oil in a large skillet and cook over medium heat, stirring often, for 2 to 3 minutes to soften. Add the seitan strips and cook and stir for 2 minutes. Stir in the garlic, tamari, and crushed red pepper flakes and season with salt and pepper to taste. Cook and stir for 1 minute longer.

To assemble each sandwich, partially split open the submarine roll. Place half of the seitan-vegetable mixture on the bottom half of the roll. Top with a slice of vegan cheese. Serve hot.

Fill and assemble the other sandwich in the same fashion if you will be serving it immediately. Store any remaining sandwich ingredients separately in the refrigerator for 3 to 5 days.

VARIATIONS

- Add sliced jalapeño chiles or other hot peppers to the sandwich filling for extra flavor and heat.
- Replace the vegan cheese with a few tablespoons of Special "Cheese" Sauce (page 47).

TIP: Save the liquid the seitan is packaged in and store it in an airtight container in the refrigerator. Use it in place of broth in soups, sauces, or casseroles.

Better Than Takeout

Single people are often tempted to swing by a restaurant or drive-thru to pick up a meal instead of cooking something for themselves, but dining out all the time can take a big bite out of your wallet and cause you to put on the pounds. Turn to this section for inspiration and assistance in preparing nutritious, homemade versions of popular menu items commonly ordered from takeout places and fast-food joints. With a little know-how, you can easily make vegan burgers, fries, nuggets, and pizza, right in your own kitchen. After mastering these classic American favorites, venture into Far Eastern cuisine and take a crack at making your own spicy Indian curry, Chinese vegetable stir-fry, and Thai noodle dishes.

Pizza Margherita was created and named for a former queen of Italy. It depicts the colors of the Italian flag—green, white, and red—and is classically made with the simple ingredients of basil, cheese, and tomatoes. In this vegan version, individual pizzas are created using whole pita breads instead of homemade dough, making them a quick and easy option when a pizza craving strikes.

pita Margherita

YIELD: 2 PITAS

2 (6-inch) **whole grain pita breads**

2 **plum tomatoes, each cut into 6 slices**

Sea salt

Freshly ground black pepper

½ cup **shredded vegan mozzarella cheese or other vegan cheese of choice**

2 tablespoons **vegan Parmesan or nutritional yeast flakes**

6 to 8 **fresh basil leaves**

Olive oil

Preheat the oven to 425 degrees F. Place the pita breads on a cookie sheet.

Decoratively layer 6 of the tomato slices atop each pita and season them with salt and pepper to taste. Top each pita with half of the shredded cheese, half of the vegan Parmesan, and 3 to 4 torn basil leaves. Drizzle a little olive oil to taste over each pita.

Bake for 5 to 7 minutes or until the pitas are crisp and lightly browned around the edges and the cheese is melted. Cut each pita into 4 pieces before serving. Serve hot.

VARIATIONS

Dress up your pizza with additional vegetable toppings, such as thinly sliced mushrooms, onions, olives, or broccoli florets, or a few slices of vegan pepperoni.

These tasty tofu strips are similar to the ever-popular fast-food nuggets, but these bite-size morsels are baked rather than deep-fried. Enjoy them as a main dish or snack, served with ketchup, maple-sweetened mustard, or any other condiments or dipping sauces you prefer.

Seasoned Tofu **tidbits**

YIELD: 2 CUPS

1 pound firm or extra-firm regular tofu

2 tablespoons tamari

1 tablespoon olive oil

¾ teaspoon garlic powder

¾ teaspoon onion powder

1 tablespoon nutritional yeast flakes

Preheat the oven to 375 degrees F. Cut the tofu into 1-inch cubes or strips and place them on a cookie sheet or in a baking pan.

Add the tamari, olive oil, garlic powder, and onion powder and stir well to evenly coat the tofu. Arrange the tofu pieces in a single layer and sprinkle them with half of the nutritional yeast flakes.

Bake for 20 minutes. Remove from the oven, stir with a metal or heatproof spatula, and spread the pieces into a single layer again. Sprinkle the remaining nutritional yeast flakes over the tofu.

Bake for 10 to 15 minutes longer or until golden brown and crisp around the edges. Serve hot.

TIP: Add Seasoned Tofu Tidbits to soups, stews, salads, pasta, and grains, or use them to make Unchicken Tofu Salad (page 58).

Who doesn't like french fries? In fact, studies show that deep-fried french fries and potato chips are often the only servings of vegetables in the daily diets of some Americans, which is really a shame. Baked french fries and potato wedges have only a fraction of the fat but are just as tasty, especially if they are well seasoned, as with this recipe.

oven-baked French Fries or potato wedges

YIELD: 2 SERVINGS

1 large russet potato or other potato of choice

1½ teaspoons olive oil

1 teaspoon nutritional yeast flakes

¼ teaspoon chili powder

¼ teaspoon garlic powder

¼ teaspoon onion powder

¼ teaspoon sea salt

⅛ teaspoon freshly ground black pepper

Preheat the oven to 375 degrees F. Cut the potato into french-fry shapes or wedges and place them on a cookie sheet or in a baking pan.

Drizzle the olive oil over the potatoes and sprinkle them with the nutritional yeast flakes and all of the seasonings. Using your hands, toss the potatoes until they are evenly coated and spread them into a single layer.

Bake for 20 minutes. Stir with a metal or heatproof spatula and spread the potatoes into a single layer again.

Bake for 20 to 25 minutes longer or until the potatoes are fork-tender and lightly browned around the edges.

VARIATIONS

- Vary the flavor of your fries by adding or substituting other spices or herbs.
- Instead of potatoes, try other root vegetables, such as garnet yams, carrots, parsnips, or beets, either individually or in combination.

Commercially made veggie burgers can be a little costly, so why not save yourself some money and mix up a batch of your own? These spicy vegan burgers are made with a colorful blend of chopped vegetables and red and black beans. They do contain quite a few ingredients, but don't let that stop you from giving them a try, as many of the ingredients are just quickly measured seasonings, flavorings, and condiments.

Tex-Mex bean burgers

YIELD: 4 BURGERS

½ cup finely diced yellow or red onions

½ cup fresh or frozen corn kernels

½ cup finely diced red bell peppers

½ cup finely diced green bell peppers

1 medium jalapeño chile, seeded and finely diced

1½ teaspoons olive oil

1 tablespoon minced garlic

½ teaspoon dried basil

½ teaspoon dried oregano

½ teaspoon chili powder

¼ teaspoon sea salt

⅛ teaspoon freshly ground black pepper

1 cup canned red beans, drained and rinsed

2 tablespoons bottled barbecue sauce, or 1 tablespoon ketchup and 1 tablespoon Dijon mustard

4 teaspoons tamari

⅔ cup rolled oats

½ cup canned black beans, drained and rinsed

4 hamburger buns, or 8 whole grain bread slices

Place the onions, corn, bell peppers, chile, and olive oil in a large skillet and cook over medium heat, stirring often, for 3 minutes to soften. Add the garlic, basil, oregano, chili powder, salt, and pepper and cook and stir for 1 to 2 minutes or until the vegetables are lightly browned. Remove from the heat.

Using a potato masher or fork, coarsely mash the red beans in a large bowl. Stir in the barbecue sauce and tamari. Add the cooked vegetables, rolled oats, and black beans and stir until well combined.

Use a ½ cup measuring cup to portion each burger patty by lightly filling and gently packing the burger mixture into the cup with the back of a spoon. Flip the cup over onto a large plate and give it a tap to release the mixture. Form each portion into a patty and chill them in the refrigerator for 30 minutes.

Lightly oil a large skillet and place it over medium heat. Arrange the patties in the hot skillet and cook them for 5 minutes or until golden brown on the bottom. Flip the patties over with a metal or heatproof spatula and cook for 5 minutes longer or until golden brown on the other side and crisp around the edges. Add additional olive oil to the skillet, if needed, to prevent the patties from sticking. Serve the burgers on buns with your choice of vegetable toppings and condiments. Stored in an airtight container in the refrigerator, leftover Tex-Mex Bean Burgers will keep for 5 to 7 days.

TIP: These burgers can be made in larger batches, precooked, and frozen in an airtight container for up to 3 months. Reheat the frozen patties in the oven or a skillet.

These tasty and versatile patties are made by blending cooked mushrooms, raw vegetables, cashews, a few seasonings, and breadcrumbs. Pair them with a salad of mixed greens and side dishes of cooked vegetables and grains, or try serving them like burgers with your choice of vegetable toppings and condiments.

savory Mushroom-Vegetable Patties

YIELD: 4 PATTIES

¾ cup chopped cremini mushrooms or other mushrooms of choice

¾ cup diced carrots

¾ cup diced yellow onions

¾ cup diced celery

½ cup raw cashews

1½ cups dry breadcrumbs

¼ cup filtered water

2 tablespoons chopped fresh parsley

2 tablespoons nutritional yeast flakes

¾ teaspoon sea salt

½ teaspoon dried thyme

½ teaspoon freshly ground black pepper

½ teaspoon cayenne

2 to 4 tablespoons whole wheat flour or spelt flour, as needed

Cook the mushrooms in a large, dry skillet over medium heat, stirring often, for 2 to 3 minutes to remove excess moisture. Remove from the heat and set aside.

Place the carrots, onions, celery, and cashews in a food processor and process for 1 to 2 minutes to finely grind the ingredients. Transfer to a medium bowl, add the mushrooms, breadcrumbs, water, parsley, nutritional yeast flakes, salt, thyme, pepper, and cayenne, and stir until well combined.

Place several tablespoons of the flour on a small plate. Using your hands, form the mixture into 4 patties. Dust the patties on all sides with the flour.

Lightly oil the same large skillet and place it over medium heat. Arrange the patties in the hot skillet and cook them for 5 minutes or until golden brown on the bottom. Flip the patties over with a metal or heatproof spatula and cook for 5 minutes longer or until golden brown on the other side and crisp around the edges. Add additional olive oil to the skillet, if needed, to prevent the patties from sticking. Serve hot. Stored in an airtight container in the refrigerator, leftover Savory Mushroom-Vegetable Patties will keep for 5 to 7 days.

You can whip up a batch of these yummy noodles covered with peanut sauce and be enjoying it in about fifteen minutes. Serve the noodles hot or cold, either plain, alongside raw or cooked vegetables, or on top of a mixed green salad.

Peanutty **noodles**

YIELD: 2 SERVINGS

8 ounces whole grain spaghetti or linguine

¼ cup unsalted smooth or crunchy peanut butter

2 tablespoons tamari

4 teaspoons toasted sesame oil

4 teaspoons freshly squeezed lime juice

2 teaspoons minced garlic

2 teaspoons minced fresh ginger

⅛ teaspoon cayenne

½ cup thinly sliced green onions

½ cup chopped fresh cilantro or parsley

¼ cup finely chopped peanuts

To cook the spaghetti, fill a large pot two-thirds full with filtered water and bring to a boil over medium-high heat. Add the spaghetti and cook, stirring occasionally, according to the time on the package instructions or until tender.

Meanwhile, place the peanut butter, tamari, toasted sesame oil, lime juice, garlic, ginger, and cayenne in a medium bowl and whisk until well combined.

Drain the spaghetti in a colander, add it to the peanut sauce, and toss until evenly coated. Add all of the remaining ingredients and toss again. Serve hot, warm, or thoroughly chilled.

VARIATIONS

If you can't have peanuts, substitute cashew butter and chopped cashews, or omit the nut-based combination altogether and add a few crushed red pepper flakes to the other sauce ingredients to transform the dish into Szechuan-style sesame noodles.

This noodle and mixed-vegetable dish, with its sweet, sour, and spicy flavor, is a popular offering at many Thai restaurants. It's usually made with white rice noodles, but using brown rice spaghetti or other whole grain noodles instead makes the dish more nutritious. Serve it either hot or cold, with a generous squeeze of fresh lime juice to heighten its flavor.

pad Thai

YIELD: 2 SERVINGS

6 ounces whole grain spaghetti

2 tablespoons freshly squeezed lime juice

4 teaspoons turbinado sugar or other sugar of choice

4 teaspoons tamari

4 teaspoons toasted sesame oil

1 tablespoon filtered water

½ teaspoon crushed red pepper flakes or hot sauce

¾ cup shredded carrots

¾ cup mung bean sprouts, rinsed

½ cup thinly sliced green onions

1 tablespoon minced garlic

1 tablespoon minced fresh ginger

⅓ cup chopped fresh cilantro

3 tablespoons finely chopped peanuts

½ lime, cut into wedges

To cook the spaghetti, fill a large pot two-thirds full with filtered water and bring to a boil over medium-high heat. Add the spaghetti and cook, stirring occasionally, according to the time on the package instructions or until tender.

Meanwhile, place the lime juice, sugar, tamari, 1 teaspoon of the toasted sesame oil, water, and crushed red pepper flakes in a small bowl and whisk until well combined. Set aside.

Drain the spaghetti in a colander and set aside. Place the carrots, mung bean sprouts, and the remaining 3 teaspoons toasted sesame oil in a large skillet and cook over medium heat for 2 minutes, stirring often. Add the green onions, garlic, and ginger and cook and stir for 1 minute.

Add the spaghetti, reserved sauce, and cilantro and cook and stir for 1 to 2 minutes or until all of the sauce is absorbed. Top with the chopped peanuts. Serve hot or cold with lime wedges, and squeeze fresh lime juice over individual servings.

VARIATIONS

Replace the spaghetti with soba noodles or packages of ramen noodles (minus their seasoning packets).

Stir-fries are made by quickly cooking ingredients in a small amount of oil, traditionally in a wok over high heat, but they can just as easily be made in a large skillet if you don't own a wok. When preparing a stir-fry, be sure to cook the vegetables only briefly so that they retain their colors and crisp textures. This vegetable-packed stir-fry gets its spicy flavor from a generous dose of jalapeño chile, garlic, ginger, and red pepper flakes. Serve it as a side dish, or as a main dish over grains or noodles.

Sizzling Sesame stir-fry

YIELD: 2 TO 3 SERVINGS

¾ cup cubed Asian eggplant (1-inch cubes)

3 teaspoons toasted sesame oil

¾ cup small broccoli florets

¾ cup thinly sliced carrots

¾ cup thinly sliced yellow or red onions

1½ cups chopped bok choy or other greens of choice

½ cup halved and thinly sliced shiitake or cremini mushrooms

½ of a medium jalapeño chile, seeded and finely diced

1 tablespoon minced garlic

1 tablespoon minced fresh ginger

1 tablespoon tamari

1 tablespoon sesame seeds

½ teaspoon crushed red pepper flakes

Sea salt

Freshly ground black pepper

Place the eggplant and 1 teaspoon of the toasted sesame oil in a large skillet and cook over medium-high heat, stirring often, for 2 minutes to soften. Add 1 teaspoon of the remaining toasted sesame oil and all of the broccoli, carrots, and onions. Cook and stir for 2 minutes.

Add the bok choy, mushrooms, chile, garlic, and ginger and cook and stir for 2 to 3 minutes or until the vegetables are crisp-tender. Add the remaining 1 teaspoon toasted sesame oil and the tamari, sesame seeds, crushed red pepper flakes, and salt and pepper to taste. Cook and stir for 1 minute. Serve hot.

VARIATIONS

Add or substitute other fresh or frozen vegetables to suit your tastes, or add cubes of seitan, tofu, or tempeh.

Indian vegetable-based stews, also known as curries, are commonly made with an assortment of vegetables and coconut milk and are liberally spiced. The flavorful combination of seasonings may even cause you to break into a cold sweat while eating it, but fear not, as many of these spices are excellent for perking up your digestion. You can control the heat of this dish by using either mild or hot curry powder. To cut down on preparation and cooking times, frozen mixed vegetables are used in place of fresh vegetables. Serve the curry over rice or other grains.

Coconut Curry **in a hurry**

YIELD: 2 TO 3 SERVINGS

2 medium red-skinned potatoes, peeled and cut into 1-inch cubes

½ cup diced yellow onions

2 teaspoons olive oil

1 tablespoon minced garlic

1 tablespoon minced fresh ginger

2 teaspoons curry powder

½ teaspoon ground cumin

¼ teaspoon sea salt

¼ teaspoon freshly ground black pepper

Pinch of cayenne

1 package (10 ounces) **frozen California mixed vegetables or other mixed vegetables of choice**

1 cup lite coconut milk

¾ cup canned chickpeas, drained and rinsed

½ cup frozen peas or edamame

½ cup filtered water

Place the potatoes, onions, and olive oil in a large pot and cook over medium heat for 4 minutes, stirring often. Add the garlic, ginger, curry powder, cumin, salt, pepper, and cayenne and cook and stir for 1 minute.

Stir in all of the remaining ingredients. Cover, reduce the heat to low, and simmer for 15 to 20 minutes or until the vegetables are tender. Taste and adjust the seasonings as desired. Serve hot.

Dishing Up Dinner

After a long day at school or work, you'll undoubtedly find yourself ravenous for a great-tasting dinner. Regardless of how hungry you are or how much energy you have left, you're sure to find something appealing in this section for your evening meal. On the stovetop, you can cook a quick pasta dish, hearty vegetable stew, or beans-and-greens combo. If you can stave off your hunger for a while, heat up the oven and bake one of the soy-based selections, a terrific meatless loaf, or a pasta casserole that is reminiscent of lasagne. You may want to make larger amounts of the seitan dish or baked soy offerings so you can enjoy them later as fillings for sandwiches or additions to other dishes for extra flavor.

Puttanesca sauce, rumor has it, originated with the Italian "ladies of the evening" and was affectionately named for them. As the story goes, they would make their tomato sauce in the early afternoon and let the aroma of the sauce waft out their windows in hopes of attracting men to visit them. No matter what the story or origin of its name, it is a quick, easy, and filling meal to prepare.

pasta Puttanesca

YIELD: 2 TO 3 SERVINGS

6 ounces whole grain pasta of choice

½ cup diced yellow or red onions

½ cup diced green bell peppers

2 teaspoons olive oil

2 teaspoons minced garlic

1 teaspoon Italian seasoning blend, or ½ teaspoon dried basil and ½ teaspoon dried oregano

¼ teaspoon crushed red pepper flakes

1 can (14 ounces) crushed tomatoes

¼ cup chopped pitted olives of choice

¼ cup chopped fresh parsley

1 tablespoon capers

Sea salt

Freshly ground black pepper

Vegan Parmesan or nutritional yeast flakes

To cook the pasta, fill a large pot two-thirds full with filtered water and bring to a boil over medium-high heat. Add the pasta and cook, stirring occasionally, according to the time on the package instructions or until tender.

Meanwhile, place the onions, bell peppers, and olive oil in a large skillet and cook over medium heat, stirring often, for 3 minutes to soften. Add the garlic, Italian seasoning, and crushed red pepper flakes and cook and stir for 1 minute. Add the tomatoes, olives, parsley, and capers and cook and stir for 2 to 3 minutes.

Drain the pasta in a colander. Add it to the sauce and stir until well combined. Season with salt and pepper to taste and remove from the heat. Serve hot. Top individual servings with vegan Parmesan as desired.

VARIATIONS

Add chopped mushrooms, Asian eggplant, or spinach to the sauce for extra flavor and to make the dish a bit heartier.

Turn to this recipe whenever your pantry or refrigerator is short on supplies, as you're bound to have at least these few ingredients on hand. This classic Italian pasta dish is affectionately known as *aglio e olio*, which literally means "garlic and oil," and is commonly enjoyed for lunch, dinner, and even a late-night snack (which is how I was first introduced to it by my Italian husband). It can be enjoyed as a stand-alone dish with some bread, or served alongside steamed vegetables or a leafy green salad for a heartier meal.

spaghetti with Garlic and Olive Oil

YIELD: 2 SERVINGS

6 ounces whole grain spaghetti or other pasta of choice

1 tablespoon minced garlic

1 tablespoon olive oil

¼ teaspoon crushed red pepper flakes

¼ teaspoon sea salt

¼ teaspoon freshly ground black pepper

Vegan Parmesan or nutritional yeast flakes

To cook the pasta, fill a large pot two-thirds full with filtered water and bring to a boil over medium-high heat. Add the spaghetti and cook, stirring occasionally, according to the time on the package instructions or until tender.

Meanwhile, place the garlic and olive oil in a small skillet and cook over medium heat, stirring often, for 1 to 2 minutes or until lightly golden and fragrant. Add the crushed red pepper flakes, salt, and pepper and cook and stir for 30 seconds. Remove from the heat.

Drain the spaghetti in a colander and return it to the pot. Add the garlic-oil mixture and toss until evenly coated. Serve hot. Top individual servings with vegan Parmesan as desired.

VARIATIONS

Add chopped fresh herbs, mushrooms, tomatoes, or spinach for extra flavor and to make the dish a bit heartier. To heighten the taste even more, add a little freshly squeezed lemon juice.

This baked pasta casserole shares many of the same components and flavors of classic Italian lasagne, but it can be made with less effort and in just a fraction of the time. It's made with ziti, which is a long, narrow, tube-shaped pasta. If you can't find ziti in your store, substitute penne or any other similarly shaped pasta. Serve this casserole with steamed vegetables or a leafy green salad.

Baked Ziti **casserole**

YIELD: 2 TO 3 SERVINGS

8 ounces whole grain ziti or other tube-shaped pasta of choice

8 ounces firm or extra-firm regular tofu

3 tablespoons nutritional yeast flakes

4 teaspoons freshly squeezed lemon juice

2 teaspoons agave nectar or brown rice syrup

2 teaspoons garlic powder

1½ teaspoons onion powder

¾ teaspoon dried basil

¾ teaspoon dried oregano

½ teaspoon sea salt

⅛ teaspoon freshly ground black pepper

1 cup stemmed and chopped spinach

2 tablespoons chopped fresh parsley

1½ cups bottled marinara sauce or other tomato sauce of choice

¼ cup shredded vegan mozzarella cheese or other vegan cheese of choice

To cook the ziti, fill a large pot two-thirds full with filtered water and bring to a boil over medium-high heat. Add the ziti and cook, stirring occasionally, according to the time on the package instructions or until tender.

Meanwhile, crumble the tofu into a large bowl using your fingers. Add the nutritional yeast flakes, lemon juice, agave nectar, garlic powder, onion powder, basil, oregano, salt, and pepper and mash with a fork until completely smooth.

Preheat the oven to 375 degrees F. Lightly oil a 9-inch square baking pan or casserole dish. Drain the ziti in a colander and add it to the tofu mixture along with the chopped spinach and parsley. Stir until well combined.

Place half of the ziti mixture into the prepared pan. Top it with half of the marinara sauce and half of the shredded cheese. Repeat the layering procedure with the remaining ziti, marinara sauce, and cheese. Sprinkle a little additional cheese or nutritional yeast flakes over the top, if desired. Bake for 30 minutes or until heated through and lightly browned around the edges. Serve hot.

VARIATIONS

- Replace the spinach with other dark leafy greens of your choice.
- Add other chopped or sliced vegetables such as broccoli, Asian eggplant, mushrooms, peppers, or zucchini.
- Add other ingredients like chopped fresh basil, sliced olives, sliced or cubed vegan sausage, or meatless meatballs.

Here's a new twist on stuffed mushrooms, which are often served as an appetizer at parties. Instead of being bite-size morsels, these are supersized with portobello mushrooms and are meant to be enjoyed as a meatless main dish. Serve them alongside cooked vegetables and grains or with a mixed greens salad for a light yet satisfying meal.

supper-size Stuffed Mushrooms

YIELD: 2 TO 3 SERVINGS

2 large or 3 medium portobello mushrooms

¼ cup finely diced yellow onions

¼ cup finely diced celery

¼ cup thinly sliced green onions

1 tablespoon olive oil

8 ounces firm or extra-firm regular tofu

1 tablespoon minced garlic

½ teaspoon dried thyme

⅓ cup dry breadcrumbs

2 tablespoons nutritional yeast flakes

2 tablespoons chopped fresh parsley

Sea salt

Freshly ground black pepper

Preheat the oven to 375 degrees F. Lightly oil a cookie sheet and set aside. Remove the stems from the mushrooms, set aside the mushroom caps, and chop the stems. Place the mushroom stems, onions, celery, green onions, and olive oil in a large skillet and cook over medium heat, stirring often, for 3 minutes to soften.

Crumble the tofu into the skillet using your fingers. Add the garlic and thyme and cook and stir for 2 to 3 minutes or until the vegetables are fork-tender. Remove the skillet from the heat. Add the breadcrumbs, nutritional yeast flakes, and parsley and stir until well combined. Season with salt and pepper to taste.

Fill the reserved mushroom caps with equal portions of the tofu mixture, slightly mounding the tops. Place the stuffed caps on the prepared cookie sheet and bake for 15 to 20 minutes or until heated through and lightly browned on top. Serve hot.

VARIATION

Make smaller stuffed mushrooms by replacing the portobellos with cremini or button mushrooms and serving them as an appetizer or snack.

Greens and beans are excellent sources of iron, calcium, low-fat protein, and fiber. You can use whatever variety of greens you have on hand, such as kale, spinach, Swiss chard, collard greens, or mustard greens. Southerners enjoy their cooked beans and greens with a little something to sop up the juices (affectionately known as pot liquor), like bread, cornbread, or biscuits. For a heartier meal you may want to try this as well, or simply serve this dish over your favorite grains.

bayou Beans and Greens

YIELD: 2 TO 3 SERVINGS

½ cup diced yellow onions

½ cup diced green bell peppers

1½ teaspoons olive oil

2 teaspoons minced garlic

1 bunch greens of choice, stemmed and chopped (6 to 8 cups)

1 can (15 ounces) red beans or other beans of choice, drained and rinsed

½ cup filtered water

2 teaspoons nutritional yeast flakes

½ teaspoon dried oregano

½ teaspoon dried thyme

¼ teaspoon sea salt

⅛ teaspoon freshly ground black pepper

Hot sauce or crushed red pepper flakes

Place the onions, bell peppers, and olive oil in a large saucepan or pot and cook over medium heat, stirring often, for 2 to 3 minutes to soften. Add the garlic and cook and stir for 1 minute.

Stir in the greens, beans, water, nutritional yeast flakes, oregano, thyme, salt, and pepper. Cover, reduce the heat to low, and simmer for 5 to 7 minutes or until the greens are tender. Taste and adjust the seasonings as desired. Serve hot. Sprinkle a little hot sauce or crushed red pepper flakes over individual servings as desired.

This skillet-cooked supper contains only a few ingredients and cooks up in minutes. The final flavor of this dish is determined by the type of seitan that you use, so depending on your mood, choose a mildly flavored one, such as teriyaki, or perhaps a spicy barbecue variety. Purchase seitan in a block or in chunks, because you will need bite-size chunks for use in this recipe. Serve this dish over cooked grains or pasta for a hearty one-plate meal, or use it as a filling for sandwiches.

savory Seitan and Vegetables

YIELD: 2 TO 3 SERVINGS

8 ounces prepackaged seitan, cut into chunks

1 large portobello mushroom, halved and thinly sliced

¾ cup small broccoli florets

¾ cup thinly sliced yellow or red onions

¾ cup thinly sliced green or red bell peppers

1 tablespoon olive oil

1 tablespoon minced garlic

1 tablespoon cold filtered water

1½ teaspoons cornstarch

Sea salt

Freshly ground black pepper

Remove the seitan from its packaging and drain off and reserve the liquid. Lightly pat the seitan dry with a paper towel. If the seitan isn't precut into chunks, cut it into bite-size pieces and set aside.

Place the mushroom, broccoli, onions, bell peppers, and olive oil in a large skillet and cook over medium heat, stirring often, for 3 minutes to soften. Add the reserved seitan chunks and cook and stir for 3 minutes or until the vegetables are tender. Add the garlic and cook and stir for 1 minute longer.

Place the water and cornstarch in a small bowl and stir until dissolved. Add the cornstarch mixture and the reserved liquid from the seitan package and cook and stir for 1 to 2 minutes or until slightly thickened. Remove from the heat and season with salt and pepper to taste. Serve hot.

VARIATIONS

Add or substitute other vegetables, such as potatoes, squashes, carrots, or greens, to suit your tastes.

Just because you've gone meatless doesn't mean you can't still enjoy delicious barbecue. Tempeh and tofu both taste great when covered with barbecue sauce and baked to perfection. Serve this as a main dish or cut it into cubes and add it to soups, stews, vegetables, pasta, or grains. Leftovers will make a tasty sandwich filling.

soy barbecue with Peppers and Onions

YIELD: 8 PIECES (3 TO 4 SERVINGS)

12 ounces tempeh, or 1 pound firm or extra-firm regular tofu

1 tablespoon olive oil

1 tablespoon tamari

1 cup bottled barbecue sauce

⅔ cup thinly sliced yellow or red onions

⅔ cup thinly sliced green bell peppers

⅔ cup thinly sliced red bell peppers

If using tempeh, cut the block into 8 pieces. If using tofu, gently squeeze the block over the sink to remove any excess water. Cut the block of tofu in half lengthwise, turn each half cut side down, and cut each half into 4 slices to yield a total of 8 pieces.

Preheat the oven to 375 degrees F. Place the tempeh or tofu pieces in a single layer in a 9-inch square baking pan or casserole dish. Stir together the olive oil and tamari in a small bowl and pour over the pieces in the pan. Flip over each piece to evenly coat all sides.

Bake for 15 minutes. Flip the pieces over with a metal or heatproof spatula and pour half of the barbecue sauce over them. Place the onions and peppers on top and cover with the remaining barbecue sauce.

Bake for 20 to 25 minutes longer or until the vegetables are fork-tender and the barbecue sauce is bubbly. Serve hot.

VARIATIONS

- Replace the tempeh or tofu with seitan chunks or sliced vegan hot dogs.
- Replace the barbecue sauce with vegan gravy.

Those of you who grew up eating Mom's meatloaf regularly are sure to enjoy this flavorful, meatless, tempeh and mushroom version. If you like, top it with a little ketchup during the last ten minutes of baking, or serve it with vegan gravy. The sliced loaf makes a satisfying main dish, or cut it into cubes to add to soups, salads, vegetables, pasta, or grains. Leftover slices can be used as a sandwich filling.

Tempeh-Mushroom loaf

YIELD: 4 TO 5 SERVINGS

1 cup diced yellow onions

2 tablespoons olive oil

1 cup chopped cremini mushrooms

2 tablespoons minced garlic

4 teaspoons balsamic vinegar

1 teaspoon onion powder

1 teaspoon dried basil

1 teaspoon dried thyme

1 teaspoon dried rosemary

½ teaspoon crushed red pepper flakes

½ teaspoon freshly ground black pepper

12 ounces tempeh

½ cup filtered water

⅓ cup whole wheat flour or spelt flour

3 tablespoons tamari

Place the onions and 1 tablespoon of the olive oil in a small skillet and cook over medium heat, stirring often, for 2 minutes to soften. Add the mushrooms and cook and stir for 3 minutes. Add the garlic, balsamic vinegar, onion powder, basil, thyme, rosemary, crushed red pepper flakes, and pepper and cook and stir for 2 minutes. Remove from the heat and set aside to cool.

Preheat the oven to 375 degrees F. Lightly oil an 8 x 4 x 2½-inch loaf pan and set aside. Crumble the tempeh into a medium bowl using your fingers. Add the mushroom mixture, the remaining 1 tablespoon olive oil, and the water, flour, and tamari. Stir until well combined.

Press the loaf mixture evenly into the prepared pan using your hands. Bake for 30 to 40 minutes or until golden brown and firm to the touch. Let cool for 5 minutes before cutting into slices. Serve hot.

In this recipe, pieces of tempeh or tofu are covered with a simple sauce that transforms into a sweet and tangy glaze when it is baked. Serve it as a main dish or side dish, or cut it into cubes, either before or after baking, and add them to soups, salads, stir-fries, pasta, or grain dishes. Leftovers can be combined with fresh vegetables for a delicious sandwich filling.

Orange-Teriyaki **tempeh or tofu**

YIELD: 8 PIECES (3 TO 4 SERVINGS)

12 ounces tempeh, or 1 pound firm or extra-firm regular tofu

¼ cup tamari

2 tablespoons brown rice vinegar or apple cider vinegar

1 tablespoon orange marmalade

4 teaspoons toasted sesame oil

4 teaspoons maple syrup or brown rice syrup

1 tablespoon minced garlic

1 tablespoon minced fresh ginger

½ teaspoon crushed red pepper flakes

If using tempeh, cut the block into 8 pieces. If using tofu, gently squeeze the block over the sink to remove any excess water. Cut the block of tofu in half lengthwise, turn each half cut side down, and cut each half into 4 slices to yield a total of 8 pieces. Place the pieces in a single layer in a 9-inch square baking pan or casserole dish.

Preheat the oven to 375 degrees F. Place all of the remaining ingredients in a small bowl and whisk them together until well combined. Pour over the pieces in the pan and flip over each piece until evenly coated on all sides.

Bake for 20 minutes. Flip the pieces over with a metal or heatproof spatula. Bake for 15 to 20 minutes longer or until most of the sauce is absorbed. Serve hot.

For this recipe, pieces of tofu are breaded using the same technique commonly used for preparing chicken or fish, and you get to decide whether they'll be baked or fried. They can be served as a main dish or side dish, or as a sandwich filling with your choice of fresh vegetables and condiments like vegan mayonnaise, mustard, or barbecue sauce.

breaded Tofu Tenders

YIELD: 8 PIECES (3 TO 4 SERVINGS)

1 pound firm or extra-firm regular tofu

⅔ cup soymilk or other nondairy milk of choice

1 tablespoon tamari

1 tablespoon freshly squeezed lemon juice

⅔ cup whole wheat flour or spelt flour

⅓ cup cornmeal or dry breadcrumbs

3 tablespoons nutritional yeast flakes

2 teaspoons Italian seasoning blend, or 1 teaspoon dried basil and 1 teaspoon dried oregano

1 teaspoon garlic powder

½ teaspoon paprika

¼ teaspoon sea salt

¼ teaspoon freshly ground black pepper

Gently squeeze the block of tofu over the sink to remove any excess water. Cut it in half lengthwise, turn each half cut side down, and cut each half into 4 slices to yield a total of 8 pieces.

Preheat the oven to 400 degrees F. Lightly oil a cookie sheet and set aside. Place the soymilk, tamari, and lemon juice in a small bowl, stir to combine, and set aside for 10 minutes to thicken.

Place the flour on a large plate. Using your hands, thoroughly dust the tofu pieces with the flour on all sides. Place the pieces on another large plate and set aside. Stir the cornmeal, nutritional yeast flakes, Italian seasoning blend, garlic powder, paprika, salt, and pepper into the flour.

Using your hands, dip each floured piece of tofu into the soymilk mixture, then into the cornmeal mixture, pressing down slightly to thoroughly coat each piece on all sides. Place the breaded pieces on the prepared cookie sheet.

Bake for 10 to 15 minutes or until the pieces are golden brown all over. Flip the pieces over with a metal or heat-proof spatula. Bake for 10 to 15 minutes longer or until the pieces are golden brown on the other side. Serve hot or cold.

Alternatively, for a crispier crust, the breaded tofu pieces can be fried in a little olive oil in a large skillet. Drain the pieces on paper towels to remove any excess oil before serving.

VARIATION

Replace the tofu with 12 ounces of tempeh, sliced.

This low-fat yet hearty stew is chock-full of vegetables and its broth is thick and creamy. It will fill you up without fattening you up. Using some frozen vegetables in the stew cuts down on the prep and cooking time. Serve it with bread or biscuits or over grains or pasta for an even heartier meal.

from the heart Vegetable Stew

YIELD: 3 TO 4 SERVINGS

½ cup diced yellow or red onions

½ cup diced celery

4 cups filtered water

2 tablespoons minced garlic

2 medium red-skinned potatoes, peeled and cut into 1-inch cubes

1 package (10 ounces) frozen California mixed vegetables or other mixed vegetables of choice

⅓ cup frozen peas

1 teaspoon dried basil

1 teaspoon dried thyme

½ teaspoon sea salt

½ teaspoon freshly ground black pepper

½ cup soymilk other nondairy milk of choice

⅓ cup whole wheat flour or other flour of choice

2 tablespoons nutritional yeast flakes

1 tablespoon tamari

Place the onions, celery, and ½ cup of the water in a large pot and cook over medium heat, stirring often, for 2 to 3 minutes to soften. Add the garlic and cook and stir for 1 minute.

Stir in an additional 2½ cups of the water along with the potatoes, frozen mixed vegetables, frozen peas, basil, thyme, salt, and pepper. Cover, reduce the heat to low, and simmer for 20 to 25 minutes or until the vegetables are tender.

Place the remaining 1 cup water in a small bowl along with the soymilk, flour, nutritional yeast flakes, and tamari and stir until well combined. Stir this mixture into the pot with the vegetables and cook for 2 to 3 minutes or until the stew thickens. Taste and adjust the seasonings as desired. Serve hot.

VARIATIONS

- Add or substitute other vegetables, such as squashes, yams, turnips, greens.
- Add cubes of seitan, tofu, or tempeh to give this stew extra body and protein.

Eggplant, tomatoes, and chickpeas are commonly found ingredients in many Mediterranean dishes, including this one, but it's the addition of curry powder that adds a little extra spice and flavor to this savory stew. Serve the stew either plain or over pasta or grains. Add a tossed salad on the side for a satisfying meal.

Eggplant and Chickpea stew

YIELD: 3 TO 4 SERVINGS

⅔ cup diced yellow onions

⅔ cup diced green bell peppers

1½ teaspoons olive oil

1 cup cubed Asian eggplant (1-inch cubes)

1 tablespoon minced garlic

1 can (15 ounces) chickpeas, drained and rinsed

1 can (14 ounces) diced tomatoes

1½ cups filtered water

1 cup fresh or frozen cut green beans

¼ cup chopped fresh parsley

1 teaspoon dried basil

1 teaspoon dried oregano

1 teaspoon curry powder

1 teaspoon sea salt

½ teaspoon freshly ground black pepper

Place the onions, bell peppers, and olive oil in a large pot and cook over medium heat, stirring often, for 2 to 3 minutes to soften. Add the eggplant and garlic and cook and stir for 2 minutes.

Stir in all of the remaining ingredients. Cover, reduce the heat to low, and simmer for 20 to 25 minutes or until the vegetables are tender. Taste and adjust the seasonings as desired. Serve hot.

VARIATIONS

Add or substitute other fresh or frozen vegetables, such as potatoes, cauliflower, broccoli, squash, or greens, to give the stew extra bulk and flavor.

Side Dish Sidekicks

The superheroes and late-night talk show hosts wouldn't be as popular or get as many laughs without their sidekicks there beside them. The same can be said for the star attractions on your plate. Entrée items seem more spectacular when paired with one or more accompanying sensational side dishes. Much like a good sauce, the recipes in this section will give your meals more oomph and flavor, as well as fill out your plate. On the stovetop, you can prepare beans, a simple applesauce, a variety of grain-based dishes, or flavorful, sweet-and-savory combinations of assorted vegetables. There are also a few recipes for oven-baked casseroles and side dishes, which you can assemble ahead of time and simply finish baking when you arrive home after a long day. Many of these recipes are quite filling, easily portable, and suitable for family gatherings and holiday meals, in case you need to make a vegan meal for yourself out of just side dishes.

Sure you can buy applesauce in jar from any grocery store, but it tastes so much better if you make it yourself. The slightly sweet flavor in this version is achieved by cooking the apples in apple juice instead of adding sugar or other sweeteners like many manufacturers do. Serve it as a warm or cold side dish or as a topping or filling for pancakes, French toast, or desserts.

Homemade Applesauce **your way**

YIELD: 2 CUPS (2 TO 3 SERVINGS)

4 cups peeled, cored, and sliced apples of choice (2 to 3)

⅔ cup apple juice

1 teaspoon ground cinnamon

Pinch of ground ginger or other spice of choice (such as ground nutmeg or cloves)

Place the apples and apple juice in a medium saucepan and bring to a boil over medium heat. Cover, reduce the heat to low, and simmer for 20 to 25 minutes or until the apples are soft.

Remove from the heat and add the cinnamon and ginger. Using a potato masher, mash the mixture as smooth or chunky as desired. Serve hot, cold, or at room temperature. Stored in a tightly sealed container, leftover Homemade Applesauce Your Way will keep for 5 to 7 days in the refrigerator or up to 3 months in the freezer.

VARIATIONS

Vary the flavor of your applesauce by adding other fresh or frozen fruits to the apples as they cook, such as pears, berries, peaches, or mangoes.

Mashed potatoes taste so much better when made with naturally buttery-tasting Yukon gold potatoes instead of boxed dehydrated potato flakes. Top these mashed potatoes with some additional margarine or vegan gravy, chopped fresh parsley or dill weed, or a little shredded vegan cheese, if you like.

marvelous Mashed Potatoes

YIELD: 2 TO 3 SERVINGS

1½ pounds Yukon gold potatoes, peeled and cut into 1-inch cubes (2 to 3 large)

3 to 4 whole garlic cloves, peeled

⅓ to ½ cup soymilk or other nondairy milk of choice

1 tablespoon nutritional yeast flakes

2 teaspoons nonhydrogenated margarine

½ teaspoon sea salt

¼ teaspoon white pepper or freshly ground black pepper

Place the potatoes and garlic cloves in a medium saucepan. Cover them with filtered water and bring to a boil over medium heat. Reduce the heat to low and simmer for 15 to 20 minutes or until the potatoes are soft. Remove from the heat.

Drain the potatoes and garlic in a colander and return them to the saucepan. Add all of the remaining ingredients. Using a potato masher, mash the mixture as smooth or chunky as desired. Taste and add additional seasoning or margarine as desired. Serve hot.

VARIATIONS

Substitute other varieties of potatoes or add carrots or turnips to the potatoes as they cook.

TIP: Save the cooking liquid from the potatoes, store it in an airtight container in the refrigerator, and use it for making soup or other savory dishes.

Scalloped potatoes, with their creamy sauce, taste like a fancy dish that took hours to create, but they are actually a cinch to make and bake up to perfection. They are often made with cream or other dairy-based sauces, but this isn't really necessary. As you will soon discover, using nondairy milk works just fine for recreating this classic American side dish.

Simple Scalloped **potatoes**

YIELD: 2 TO 3 SERVINGS

4 cups thinly sliced red-skinned potatoes (3 to 4 medium)

½ cup finely diced red onions

2 tablespoons nutritional yeast flakes

Sea salt

Freshly ground black pepper

1¼ cups soymilk or other nondairy milk of choice

1½ teaspoons olive oil

Paprika

Preheat the oven to 375 degrees F. Lightly oil a 9-inch square baking pan or casserole dish. Layer half of the sliced potatoes, half of the chopped onions, and half of the nutritional yeast flakes into the baking pan. Season the top layer with a little salt and pepper to taste. Layer the remaining potatoes, onions, and nutritional yeast into the pan, and season the final layer with salt and pepper to taste.

Pour the soymilk over the top and shake the pan gently to allow some of it to sink to the bottom of the pan. Drizzle the olive oil over the top and sprinkle with a little paprika for extra color and flavor. Bake for 45 to 60 minutes or until the potatoes are fork-tender. Serve hot.

VARIATIONS

Substitute other varieties of potatoes or replace the potatoes with sliced carrots, turnips, rutabagas, or winter squashes.

Bread stuffing is a popular side dish that often graces the table at family gatherings, especially during the winter holidays. However, it's really a simple dish to prepare, which makes it easy to enjoy all year round.

oven-baked Bread Stuffing

YIELD: 2 TO 3 SERVINGS

¾ cup diced celery

½ cup diced yellow onions

2 teaspoons olive oil

4 to 6 slices whole grain bread, cut into 1-inch cubes (6 cups)

¼ cup chopped fresh parsley

1 tablespoon nutritional yeast flakes

1½ teaspoons dried thyme

1½ teaspoons rubbed sage

¾ teaspoon sea salt

½ teaspoon freshly ground black pepper

1½ cups filtered water or vegetable broth

1 tablespoon tamari

Preheat the oven to 375 degrees F. Lightly oil a 9-inch square baking pan or casserole dish and set aside. Place the celery, onions, and olive oil in a small skillet and cook over medium heat, stirring often, for 5 minutes or until soft. Remove from the heat.

Place the bread cubes, parsley, nutritional yeast flakes, thyme, sage, salt, and pepper in a large bowl. Add the celery-onion mixture and toss until well combined. Gently stir in the water and tamari to moisten the bread cubes.

Transfer to the prepared baking pan. Bake for 25 to 30 minutes or until the stuffing is slightly dry and browned on top. Serve hot.

VARIATIONS

- For extra flavor and texture, add chopped mushrooms or nuts to the stuffing mixture prior to baking.
- To transform this side dish into a filling entrée, use the stuffing mixture to fill hollowed-out winter squashes, such as acorn or butternut squash. Bake until the squash is fork-tender.

Yams are often served as part of the fall and winter holiday feasts, but because they are available year-round, there's really no reason you can't enjoy them more frequently. They're rich in beta-carotene and vitamin C, so feel free to swap them for mashed potatoes on your plate anytime. These yams are especially delicious served alongside grain dishes and lentils.

Yummy yams

YIELD: 3 CUPS (2 TO 3 SERVINGS)

2 to 3 large garnet yams, peeled and cut into 1-inch cubes (4 to 5 cups)

2 tablespoons soymilk or other nondairy milk of choice

½ teaspoon ground cinnamon

½ teaspoon ground ginger

½ teaspoon vanilla extract

¼ teaspoon sea salt

Place a steamer basket inside a large pot and fill the pot with 1 to 2 inches of water (the water should not touch the steamer basket). Place the yams in the steamer basket, cover the pot, and bring the water to a simmer over medium heat. Steam the yams for 15 to 20 minutes or until soft.

Remove from the heat and transfer the yams to a large bowl. Add all of the remaining ingredients. Using a potato masher, mash the mixture as smooth or chunky as desired. Serve hot.

VARIATION

Substitute peeled and cubed winter squashes, rutabagas, or carrots for the yams.

TIP: Instead of steaming the yams, boil them in filtered water until fork-tender. Drain well.

Cooked greens are a staple at most meals and family gatherings in the South, and rightfully so, as they are rich in fiber, protein, calcium, and B vitamins. You can use whichever variety of greens you have on hand, such as kale, spinach, Swiss chard, collard greens, or mustard greens. Enjoy these succulent greens with cooked beans and grains for a filling meal. You can also transform these greens into tasty sandwiches by serving them on toasted slices of bread or rolls along with slices of vegan cheese or baked tofu or tempeh.

Southern-Style greens

YIELD: 2 SERVINGS

½ cup thinly sliced yellow or red onions

1 tablespoon thinly sliced garlic

1½ teaspoons olive oil

1 bunch greens of choice, stemmed and chopped (6 to 8 cups)

Sea salt

Freshly ground black pepper

Crushed red pepper flakes or hot sauce

Place the onions, garlic, and olive oil in a large skillet and cook over medium heat, stirring often, for 2 minutes to soften. Add the greens to the skillet in batches, stirring often to help them wilt, and cook and stir for several minutes until tender. Season with salt, pepper, and crushed red pepper flakes to taste. Serve hot.

Sure, you can open up a can of beans and eat them as is, straight from the can. However, taking a little extra time to cook them with onions, garlic, and seasonings will give them much more flavor. Use any kind of beans you like, such as cannellini, pinto, red, black, or even black-eyed peas or lentils. Serve them alongside cooked grains and vegetables for a satisfying meal.

savory Stewed Beans

YIELD: 2 SERVINGS

½ cup diced yellow onions

1½ teaspoons olive oil

1 tablespoon minced garlic

1 can (15 ounces) beans of choice, drained and rinsed

½ cup filtered water

1 bay leaf

½ teaspoon dried basil

½ teaspoon dried thyme

½ teaspoon sea salt

¼ teaspoon freshly ground black pepper

¼ teaspoon crushed red pepper flakes (optional)

Place the onions and olive oil in a medium saucepan and cook over medium heat, stirring often, for 2 minutes to soften. Add the garlic and cook and stir for 1 minute. Add all of the remaining ingredients and cook and stir for 5 minutes. Remove and discard the bay leaf. Taste and adjust the seasonings as desired. Serve hot.

VARIATIONS

Replace the herbs with other herbs and spices, such as dill weed, rosemary, chili powder, curry powder, or ground ginger.

A seasoned breadcrumb topping brings Italian flair and a lot of flavor to this baked vegetable side dish. Serve it alongside pasta or grains. You can also use it to create delicious sandwiches by placing servings on toasted slices of bread or rolls and topping it with a drizzle of olive oil or a generous smear of Herb-Walnut Pesto (page 41).

vegetable Gratin

YIELD: 2 SERVINGS

2 medium yellow squashes, each cut into 6 slices (about 2 cups)

2 medium zucchinis, each cut into 6 slices (about 2 cups)

2 plum tomatoes, each cut into 6 slices (about 1⅓ cups)

½ teaspoon garlic powder

Sea salt

Freshly ground black pepper

3 tablespoons dry breadcrumbs

4 teaspoons nutritional yeast flakes or vegan Parmesan

1 teaspoon Italian seasoning blend, or ½ teaspoon dried basil and ½ teaspoon dried oregano

¼ teaspoon crushed red pepper flakes

Preheat the oven to 375 degrees F. Lightly oil a 9-inch square baking pan. Layer the yellow squashes, zucchinis, and tomatoes alternately in the pan. Sprinkle the vegetables with ¼ teaspoon of the garlic powder and salt and pepper to taste.

Place the breadcrumbs, nutritional yeast flakes, Italian seasoning blend, crushed red pepper flakes, and the remaining ¼ teaspoon garlic powder in a small bowl and stir until well combined. Sprinkle the mixture over the vegetables. Bake for 15 to 20 minutes or until the vegetables are tender and the breadcrumbs are lightly browned on top. Serve hot.

VARIATIONS

- Replace one or both of the yellow squashes with 1 or 2 medium Asian eggplants.
- Replace the vegetables in the recipe with fresh or frozen vegetables or vegetable combinations, such as broccoli, cauliflower, carrots, Brussels sprouts, or green beans.

Oven-roasting vegetables is a quick and easy way to prepare them and really brings out their flavors and natural sweetness. Feel free to express your own culinary creativity by using whichever vegetables are seasonally available or those that you have on hand, and change the ethnic flavor and flair of your dish by varying the herbs and oils that you use. These vegetables can be served as a side dish, added to pasta or grain dishes, or used as a filling for sandwiches or tortillas.

Seasonal Roasted **vegetables**

YIELD: 2 SERVINGS

4 cups sliced assorted vegetables of choice (see tip)

1 tablespoon olive oil

2 teaspoons minced garlic

1 to 2 teaspoons dried herbs or spices of choice

Sea salt

Freshly ground black pepper

Preheat the oven to 425 degrees F. Place the cut vegetables on a cookie sheet or in a baking pan and drizzle the olive oil over them. Add the garlic, herbs, and salt and pepper to taste. Using your hands, toss the vegetables until they are evenly coated, then spread them into a single layer.

Bake for 20 minutes. Stir the vegetables with a metal or heatproof spatula, and spread them out to form a single layer again.

Bake for 10 to 15 minutes longer or until the vegetables are tender and lightly browned around the edges. Serve hot.

TIP: If you prefer, the vegetables may be cut into 1-inch cubes rather than sliced.

This tomato-flavored couscous is so fast and easy to make that you will be enjoying it in no time. It's a nutritious side dish to turn to when you're pressed for time, because as the couscous cooks, you can quickly chop and assemble the other ingredients. You can turn it into a one-plate meal by serving it on mixed greens or transform it into a sandwich by stuffing it into pita bread or wrapping it in tortillas along with lettuce leaves.

Sun-Dried Tomato couscous

YIELD: 2 TO 3 SERVINGS

2 cups filtered water

¼ cup sun-dried tomato pieces

1 tablespoon minced garlic

1½ teaspoons Italian seasoning blend, or ¾ teaspoon dried basil and ¾ teaspoon dried oregano

½ teaspoon sea salt

¼ teaspoon freshly ground black pepper

1 cup whole wheat couscous

2 tablespoons pine nuts

¾ cup canned chickpeas or other beans of choice, drained and rinsed

½ cup diced zucchini

⅓ cup thinly sliced green onions

⅓ cup chopped fresh parsley

2 teaspoons olive oil

Place the water, sun-dried tomato pieces, garlic, Italian seasoning blend, salt, and pepper in a medium saucepan and bring to a boil. Stir in the couscous. Cover, remove from the heat, and set aside for 5 minutes to allow the couscous to cook.

Meanwhile, toast the pine nuts in a small skillet over medium heat, stirring often, for 1 to 2 minutes or until lightly colored and fragrant. Transfer to a small bowl.

Fluff the couscous with a fork to loosen the grains. Stir in the toasted pine nuts, chickpeas, zucchini, green onions, parsley, and olive oil. Serve hot, cold, or at room temperature.

Save yourself time by letting the bulgur soak in the refrigerator while you are away or overnight while you sleep. Then, you can quickly finish the dish by adding the other ingredients whenever you like. Baby arugula, which has a spicy, almost peppery flavor, can be purchased prepackaged and prewashed all year round, which will make your preparation of this dish even easier. You can turn this into a one-plate meal by serving it on mixed greens, or transform it into a sandwich by stuffing it into pita bread or wrapping it in tortillas with additional baby arugula or lettuce leaves.

lemon Bulgur and Broccoli

YIELD: 2 TO 3 SERVINGS

1 cup boiling filtered water

1 cup bulgur

Zest of ½ medium lemon (about 1 tablespoon)

Juice of ½ medium lemon (1 to 2 tablespoons)

1 tablespoon minced garlic

½ teaspoon sea salt

¼ teaspoon freshly ground black pepper

1½ cups prewashed, bagged baby arugula

1 cup small broccoli florets

½ cup diced red or orange bell peppers

¼ cup thinly sliced green onions

¼ cup chopped fresh dill weed or parsley

2 teaspoons olive oil

P lace the water, bulgur, lemon zest, lemon juice, garlic, salt, and pepper in a large bowl. Stir until evenly combined, cover, and set aside for 25 to 30 minutes or until all of the liquid is absorbed and the bulgur is tender.

Fluff the bulgur with a fork to loosen the grains. Stir in all of the remaining ingredients. Serve hot, cold, or at room temperature.

VARIATION

If you don't like arugula, substitute an equal amount of other baby greens of your choice.

TIPS

- It is easier to remove the zest from citrus fruits before squeezing out the juice.
- Citrus fruits at room temperature will release more of their juices.

This side dish features many commonly used south-of-the-border ingredients like corn, peppers, cilantro, and pumpkin seeds, and their flavors blend beautifully with cooked quinoa. You can serve it on a bed of mixed greens or wrap it in tortillas along with lettuce leaves and slices of avocado or tomatoes.

Mexican Maize and Quinoa medley

YIELD: 2 TO 3 SERVINGS

2 cups filtered water

1 cup quinoa, well rinsed

3 tablespoons raw pumpkin seeds

⅓ cup diced red or orange bell peppers

⅓ cup diced green bell peppers

⅔ cup fresh or frozen corn kernels

3 teaspoons olive oil

⅓ cup thinly sliced green onions

1 tablespoon minced garlic

2 tablespoons chopped pitted olives of choice

2 tablespoons chopped fresh cilantro or parsley

1 tablespoon freshly squeezed lime juice

½ teaspoon sea salt

¼ teaspoon freshly ground black pepper

Place the water and quinoa in a medium saucepan and bring to a boil. Cover, reduce the heat to low, and simmer for 10 to 15 minutes or until all of the water is absorbed.

Meanwhile, toast the pumpkin seeds in a small skillet over medium heat, stirring often, for 3 to 4 minutes or until lightly colored and fragrant. Transfer to a small bowl.

In the same skillet, cook the bell peppers and corn in 1½ teaspoons of the olive oil over medium heat, stirring often, for 3 to 4 minutes to soften. Add the green onions and garlic and cook and stir for 1 minute longer. Remove from the heat.

Fluff the quinoa with a fork to loosen the grains. Stir in the cooked vegetables, toasted pumpkin seeds, the remaining 1½ teaspoons olive oil, and the olives, cilantro, lime juice, salt, and pepper. Serve hot, cold, or at room temperature.

A generous blend of seasonings gives this grain dish a vibrant golden hue. A burst of bright green from peas, green onions, and parsley further heightens the color of this dish, while the other ingredients impart an exotic Indian flavor. It's a wonderful accompaniment to slices of baked tofu or tempeh and a leafy green salad. You can also use it as a filling for hollowed-out peppers, tomatoes, or other vegetables.

golden grains with Peas and Cashews

YIELD: 2 TO 3 SERVINGS

1⅓ cups filtered water

⅔ cup brown basmati rice or millet

1 tablespoon minced garlic

1 teaspoon curry powder

½ teaspoon ground cinnamon

½ teaspoon ground coriander

½ teaspoon sea salt

¼ teaspoon ground cloves

¼ teaspoon freshly ground black pepper

½ cup raw cashews

½ cup frozen peas, thawed

⅓ cup thinly sliced green onions

⅓ cup chopped fresh parsley

¼ cup dried currants

2 teaspoons toasted sesame oil

Place the water, rice, garlic, curry powder, cinnamon, coriander, salt, cloves, and pepper in a medium saucepan and bring to a boil. Cover, reduce the heat to low, and simmer for 25 to 35 minutes or until all of the water is absorbed. Remove from the heat and set aside, covered, for 5 minutes to allow the rice to steam.

Meanwhile, toast the cashews in a small skillet over medium heat, stirring often, for 3 to 4 minutes or until lightly colored and fragrant. Transfer to a small bowl.

Fluff the rice with a fork to loosen the grains. Stir in the toasted cashews, peas, green onions, parsley, currants, and toasted sesame oil. Serve hot, cold, or at room temperature.

TIP: If you are using millet, follow the same cooking directions and times as listed for the rice.

A humble pot of cooked rice can be transformed into a savory side dish with the addition of cooked vegetables, toasted nuts, and seasonings. This pilaf is excellent paired with slices of baked tofu or tempeh and green beans or other cooked vegetables. Serve it either hot or cold as a side dish or as a salad on mixed greens, or use it as a filling for baked winter squashes or other vegetables.

savory Wild Rice pilaf

YIELD: 2 TO 3 SERVINGS

⅓ cup chopped nuts of choice

⅔ cup mixed wild rice and grain blend of choice

⅓ cup finely diced celery

1 tablespoon toasted sesame oil

¼ cup thinly sliced green onions

2 teaspoons minced garlic

1 teaspoon dried thyme

½ teaspoon rubbed sage

½ teaspoon sea salt

¼ teaspoon freshly ground black pepper

1⅓ cups filtered water

¼ cup chopped fresh parsley

1 tablespoon tamari

Place the nuts in a medium saucepan and toast them over medium heat, stirring often, for 3 to 4 minutes or until lightly colored and fragrant. Transfer to a small bowl and set aside.

Place the mixed wild rice and grain blend, celery, and toasted sesame oil in the same saucepan and cook over medium heat, stirring often, for 2 minutes to soften. Add the green onions, garlic, thyme, sage, and pepper and cook and stir for 1 minute.

Add the water and bring to a boil over high heat. Cover, reduce the heat to low, and simmer for 40 to 45 minutes or until all of the water is absorbed. Remove from the heat and set aside, covered, for 5 minutes to allow the rice to steam.

Fluff the rice with a fork to loosen the grains. Stir in the reserved nuts and the parsley and tamari. Serve hot, cold, or at room temperature.

Baking Basics

Many people are confident when it comes to cooking, yet they feel intimidated by baking. Add not using eggs or dairy to the equation, and they become even more apprehensive. But you needn't worry, because once you get the hang of it, vegan baking can be quite fun. Plus, after all of your toiling in the kitchen, you'll get to sample the sweet treats of your labor. Yes, there are many wonderful companies selling ready-made vegan baked goods, but they can be quite expensive, especially if they are ordered by mail or over the Internet, so why not make your own for just a fraction of the price? In this section, you'll find vegan versions of many of your all-time favorite baked goods, each one simple to make and sure to rid you of any fear that you may have of baking. Try your hand with one of the quick breads or whip up a batch of biscuits, brownies, or cookies. You will also learn how to make three terrific types of cakes and a simple and creamy vegan frosting. Be sure to share your creations with family and friends; they're bound to be surprised that these delicious baked goods are egg and dairy free.

Many people lazily reach for that tube of premade biscuits found in the refrigerated cases of many grocery stores, but it doesn't take much time or effort to whip up a batch of biscuits yourself. Begin the process by souring the soymilk; this, combined with a little sugar, will give your biscuits a rich flavor, and baking powder will help them rise. Serve them hot, either plain or with your choice of toppings, such as fruit jelly or jam, maple syrup, or margarine.

golden Home-Style Biscuits

YIELD: 4 BISCUITS

¼ cup soymilk or other nondairy milk of choice

2 teaspoons freshly squeezed lemon juice or apple cider vinegar

1 cup whole wheat pastry flour

1 tablespoon unbleached cane sugar or beet sugar

2 teaspoons aluminum-free baking powder

¼ teaspoon sea salt

2 tablespoons safflower oil

Place the soymilk and lemon juice in a small bowl or measuring cup, stir to combine, and set aside for 10 minutes to thicken. Preheat the oven to 400 degrees F. Lightly oil a cookie sheet or line it with parchment paper (for easier cleanup) and set aside.

Place the flour, sugar, baking powder, and salt in a medium bowl and stir until well combined. Add the soymilk mixture and safflower oil and stir until well combined and a ball of dough is formed.

Transfer the dough to a floured work surface. Using your hands, knead the dough for 1 minute. Pat the dough into a ½-inch-thick square and cut it into 4 equal pieces.

Place the biscuits on the prepared cookie sheet. Bake for 10 to 12 minutes or until golden brown on the bottom and around the edges. Serve hot, warm, or at room temperature. Stored in an airtight container at room temperature, Golden Home-Style Biscuits will keep for 3 to 5 days.

VARIATIONS

Mix 2 to 4 tablespoons of chopped fresh herbs or shredded vegan cheese into the biscuit dough.

This cornbread can be mixed and in the oven within minutes. Serve pieces split and topped with margarine, maple syrup, or even salsa. Cornbread is especially delicious when paired with a hearty bowl of soup, stew, or chili.

quick Cornbread

YIELD: 9 PIECES

1 cup soymilk or other nondairy milk of choice

⅔ cup filtered water

¼ cup safflower oil

1¼ cups cornmeal

1 cup whole wheat pastry flour

4 teaspoons aluminum-free baking powder

1 tablespoon nutritional yeast flakes

1 tablespoon unbleached cane sugar or beet sugar

½ teaspoon sea salt

Preheat the oven to 375 degrees F. Lightly oil a 9-inch square baking pan and set aside. Place the soymilk, water, and safflower oil in a small bowl or measuring cup and stir until well combined. Place all of the remaining ingredients in a medium bowl and stir until well combined. Pour the wet ingredients into the dry ingredients and stir until well combined.

Transfer the batter to the prepared pan. Bake for 20 to 25 minutes or until a toothpick inserted in the center comes out clean. Allow the cornbread to cool slightly before cutting. Serve warm or at room temperature. Stored in an airtight container at room temperature, Quick Cornbread will keep for 3 to 5 days.

VARIATIONS

- Add 2 to 4 tablespoons of fresh or frozen corn kernels, sliced green onions, and/or chopped jalapeño chiles to the batter prior to baking.
- For muffins, spoon the batter into oiled or paper-lined muffin tins, filling them two-thirds full. Bake at 425 degrees F for 15 to 20 minutes or until lightly browned around the edges.

Mashed bananas add both flavor and moisture to this vegan quick bread recipe, and the aroma as it bakes will drive you bananas with anticipation. Enjoy slices for breakfast or dessert or as a snack.

Banana Nut **bread**

YIELD: 8 TO 10 SLICES

1½ cups whole wheat pastry flour

⅔ cup unbleached cane sugar or beet sugar

2 teaspoons baking soda

1 teaspoon ground cinnamon

¼ teaspoon ground ginger

¼ teaspoon sea salt

1 large banana, coarsely mashed (⅔ to ¾ cup)

½ cup filtered water

2 tablespoons olive oil or safflower oil

1 tablespoon apple cider vinegar

1 teaspoon vanilla extract

⅓ cup finely chopped nuts of choice

Preheat the oven to 350 degrees F. Lightly oil an 8 x 4 x 2½-inch loaf pan and set aside. Place the flour, sugar, baking soda, cinnamon, ginger, and salt in a medium bowl and whisk until well combined. Whisk in the banana, water, oil, vinegar, and vanilla extract.

Transfer the batter to the prepared pan. Sprinkle the chopped nuts over the top and press them in gently with your hand.

Bake for 20 to 25 minutes or until a toothpick inserted in the center comes out clean. Allow the loaf to cool slightly before cutting it. Serve hot, warm, or at room temperature. Stored in an airtight container at room temperature, Banana Nut Bread will keep for 3 to 5 days.

VARIATIONS

Add other ingredients to the batter, such as vegan chocolate or carob chips, fresh or frozen berries, or chopped fresh or dried fruit.

These chocolate chip cookies are made with barley and oat flour, making them suitable for those who suffer from wheat sensitivities. Enjoy them as a dessert or snack. If you like, dip them into soymilk or coffee or crumble them into a bowlful of nondairy ice cream.

wheat-free Chocolate Chip Cookies

YIELD: 8 TO 9 COOKIES

½ cup barley flour

½ cup oat flour

¼ teaspoon aluminum-free baking powder

¼ teaspoon baking soda

¼ teaspoon sea salt

⅓ cup maple syrup or brown rice syrup

3 tablespoons olive oil or safflower oil

½ teaspoon vanilla extract

⅓ cup vegan chocolate chips, or ¼ cup coarsely chopped vegan chocolate bar

Preheat the oven to 350 degrees F. Lightly oil a cookie sheet or line it with parchment paper (for easier cleanup) and set aside. Place the barley flour, oat flour, baking powder, baking soda, and salt in a medium bowl and stir until well combined. Add the maple syrup, oil, and vanilla extract and stir until well combined to form a soft dough. Stir in the chocolate chips.

Portion the cookie dough by tablespoonfuls onto the prepared cookie sheet, spacing them 2 inches apart. Bake for 12 to 15 minutes or until golden brown on the bottom and around the edges. Allow the cookies to cool on the cookie sheet for 2 minutes before transferring them to a rack to cool completely. Stored in an airtight container at room temperature, Wheat-Free Chocolate Chip Cookies will keep for 5 to 7 days.

TIP: If you can't find oat flour at your local store, you can make your own by pulverizing rolled oats in a blender or food processor.

Fresh orange juice and zest are used to add moisture to the raisins in these spiced oatmeal cookies, as well as a little extra sweetness and flavor. Enjoy these cookies as a dessert or snack. If you like, dip them into soymilk, tea, or coffee.

orange-spiced Oatmeal Raisin Cookies

YIELD: 8 TO 9 COOKIES

¼ cup raisins

Zest of ½ medium orange (1 to 2 tablespoons)

Juice of ½ medium orange (3 to 4 tablespoons)

3 tablespoons nonhydrogenated margarine

3 tablespoons unbleached cane sugar or beet sugar

½ teaspoon vanilla extract

½ cup rolled oats

⅓ cup whole wheat pastry flour or spelt flour

¼ teaspoon baking soda

¼ teaspoon ground cinnamon

⅛ teaspoon ground ginger

Place the raisins, orange zest, and orange juice in a small bowl and let rest for 30 minutes to plump the raisins. Preheat the oven to 350 degrees F. Lightly oil a cookie sheet or line it with parchment paper (for easier cleanup) and set aside.

Place the margarine, sugar, and vanilla extract in a medium bowl and stir until well combined. Add the raisin mixture, rolled oats, flour, baking soda, cinnamon, and ginger and stir until well combined to form a soft dough.

Portion the cookie dough by tablespoonfuls onto the prepared cookie sheet, spacing them 2 inches apart. Flatten each cookie slightly with wet fingers.

Bake for 12 minutes or until golden brown on the bottom and around the edges. Allow the cookies to cool on the cookie sheet for 2 minutes before transferring them to a rack to cool completely. Stored in an airtight container at room temperature, Orange-Spiced Oatmeal Raisin Cookies will keep for 5 to 7 days.

VARIATIONS

- Substitute other varieties of dried fruit.
- Add chopped nuts or seeds.

Peanut butter cookies with cute crisscross patterns etched into their tops are a childhood favorite that most of us never outgrow. And why shouldn't they be? In addition to being an excellent source of plant-based protein, peanut butter tastes great, especially in these delicious, crunchy cookies.

classic Peanut Butter Cookies

YIELD: 8 TO 9 COOKIES

⅓ cup unbleached cane sugar or beet sugar

3 tablespoons unsalted smooth or crunchy peanut butter

2 tablespoons nonhydrogenated margarine

4 teaspoons filtered water

½ teaspoon vanilla extract

½ cup whole wheat pastry flour

¼ teaspoon baking soda

¼ teaspoon sea salt

Preheat the oven to 375 degrees F. Lightly oil a cookie sheet or line it with parchment paper (for easier cleanup) and set aside. Place the sugar, peanut butter, margarine, water, and vanilla extract in a medium bowl and stir until well combined. Add the flour, baking soda, and salt and stir until well combined to form a soft dough.

Portion the cookie dough by tablespoonfuls onto the prepared cookie sheet, spacing them 2 inches apart. Flatten each cookie slightly in a crisscross pattern with the tines of a fork dipped in flour.

Bake for 8 minutes or until golden brown on the bottom and around the edges. Allow the cookies to cool on the cookie sheet for 2 minutes before transferring them to a rack to cool completely. Stored in an airtight container at room temperature, Classic Peanut Butter Cookies will keep for 5 to 7 days.

TIP: If you can't have peanuts, substitute cashew butter, almond butter, hazelnut butter, roasted soy nut butter, or any other nut butter you prefer.

No need to stop by the bakery or reach for a boxed mix when you find yourself in the mood for some brownies. Just make them yourself the old-fashioned way! These brownies bake up moist, rich, and chocolaty thanks to a combination of cocoa powder, chocolate chips, and a surprising ingredient—puréed bananas—which are used as a great-tasting egg replacement in this recipe.

Double Chocolate brownies

YIELD: 9 BROWNIES

1 cup vegan chocolate chips

2 tablespoons nonhydrogenated margarine

1 large banana

4 teaspoons filtered water

½ teaspoon vanilla extract

⅔ cup whole wheat pastry flour

½ cup unbleached cane sugar or beet sugar

¼ cup cocoa powder

¼ teaspoon aluminum-free baking powder

¼ teaspoon sea salt

VARIATION

For a hot fudge brownie sundae, place a brownie in a bowl and top with a scoop of nondairy ice cream or sorbet and a little Hot Fudge Sauce (page 126).

Improvise a double boiler to melt the chocolate chips by using a small saucepan and a small or medium glass or metal bowl (the bowl should be large enough to rest on top of the saucepan). Fill the saucepan halfway with water and bring to a simmer over low heat. Place the bowl on the top of the saucepan. Add the chocolate chips and margarine and heat until the chocolate chips are thoroughly melted. Remove from the heat and set aside.

Alternatively, melt the chocolate chips and margarine in a glass bowl in a microwave oven. Heat for 30 seconds at a time until the chocolate chips begin to melt. Remove from the microwave oven, stir, and set aside.

Break the banana into quarters and place it in a food processor or blender along with the water and vanilla extract. Process for 1 minute. Scrape down the sides of the container and process for 1 minute longer or until completely smooth.

Preheat the oven to 350 degrees F. Lightly oil a 9-inch square baking pan and set aside. Place the flour, sugar, cocoa powder, baking powder, and salt in a medium bowl and stir until well combined. Stir in the banana mixture and mix well. Stir in the melted chocolate chip mixture until well combined.

Transfer the batter to the prepared pan. Bake for 30 to 40 minutes or until set in the center. Do not check for doneness with an inserted toothpick. Allow the brownies to cool completely for at least 1 hour or longer before cutting them into squares. Stored in an airtight container at room temperature, Double Chocolate Brownies will keep for 3 to 5 days.

This light and fluffy vegan frosting closely resembles classic buttercream frosting, which is typically made by beating together butter and powdered sugar. It works well for frosting and piping on top of cakes, cupcakes, and desserts.

fluffy Vegan Frosting

YIELD: 1¼ CUPS (ENOUGH TO FROST THE TOP AND SIDES OF ONE 9-INCH CAKE LAYER)

¼ cup nonhydrogenated margarine

1 tablespoon soymilk or other nondairy milk of choice

1½ cups vegan powdered sugar

¾ teaspoon vanilla extract

Place the margarine and soymilk in a medium bowl. Beat them together using an electric mixer or whisk for 30 seconds to soften. Add the powdered sugar and vanilla extract and beat for 1 to 2 minutes or until light and fluffy. Use immediately or chill in the refrigerator. Stored in an airtight container in the refrigerator, Fluffy Vegan Frosting will keep for 5 to 7 days.

VARIATIONS

Modify the flavor and color of this frosting by adding other ingredients, such as additional flavoring extracts, mashed fruit or berries, or cocoa or carob powder.

TIP: This recipe can be doubled or tripled to make enough frosting for multiple layers or larger cakes.

You don't need dairy products or lots of fat to make a delicious and moist cake, as this recipe demonstrates. The cake can be served plain, frosted with Fluffy Vegan Frosting (page 118), dusted with a little vegan powdered sugar, or topped with fresh fruit or berries and a scoop of sorbet.

Light and Luscious **lemon cake**

YIELD: 9 PIECES

1½ cups whole wheat pastry flour

¾ cup unbleached cane sugar or beet sugar

1½ teaspoons baking soda

¼ teaspoon sea salt

Zest of 2 medium lemons (3 to 4 tablespoons)

Juice of 2 medium lemons (⅓ to ½ cup)

¼ cup filtered water

2 tablespoons olive oil or safflower oil

1 tablespoon apple cider vinegar

1 teaspoon vanilla extract

Preheat the oven to 350 degrees F. Lightly oil a 9-inch round or square baking pan and set aside. Place the flour, sugar, baking soda, and salt in a medium bowl and whisk until well combined. Place the lemon zest, lemon juice, water, oil, vinegar, and vanilla extract in a small bowl and whisk until well combined. Whisk the wet ingredients into the dry ingredients until completely smooth.

Transfer the batter to the prepared pan. Bake for 20 to 25 minutes or until a toothpick inserted in the center comes out clean. Allow the cake to cool completely before cutting or frosting. Stored in an airtight container at room temperature, Light and Luscious Lemon Cake will keep for 3 to 5 days.

VEGAN VANILLA CAKE

Omit the lemon zest and juice and add ⅓ cup soymilk and an additional ½ to 1 teaspoon vanilla extract. Bake according to the recipe instructions.

TIP: To make a two-layer cake, double the ingredients and bake the batter using two 9-inch cake pans. This amount of batter can also be used to make a 9 x 13-inch cake. Make a double batch of frosting if you are going to frost these larger cakes.

"Dark and rich" best describes this vegan chocolate cake, which is sweetened with maple syrup or agave nectar instead of sugar. It is sure to please any die-hard chocoholic. Enjoy it either plain or frosted with Fluffy Vegan Frosting (page 118) or one of its variations. Alternatively, drizzle slices with warm Hot Fudge Sauce (page 126).

rich dark Chocolate Cake

YIELD: 9 PIECES

1¼ cups whole wheat pastry flour

¾ cup cocoa powder

1 teaspoon aluminum-free baking powder

¾ teaspoon baking soda

⅛ teaspoon sea salt

⅔ cup soymilk or other nondairy milk of choice

⅔ cup filtered water

⅔ cup maple syrup or agave nectar

¼ cup olive oil or safflower oil

4 ounces firm or extra-firm silken tofu (about ½ cup)

1 teaspoon apple cider vinegar

1 teaspoon vanilla extract

Preheat the oven to 350 degrees F. Lightly oil a 9-inch round or square baking pan and set aside. Place the flour, cocoa powder, baking powder, baking soda, and salt in a medium bowl and whisk until well combined.

Place the soymilk, water, maple syrup, oil, tofu, vinegar, and vanilla extract in a food processor or blender and process for 1 minute or until completely smooth. Whisk the wet ingredients into the dry ingredients until completely smooth.

Transfer the batter to the prepared pan. Bake for 45 to 55 minutes or until a toothpick inserted in the center comes out clean. Allow the cake to cool completely before cutting or frosting. Stored in an airtight container at room temperature, Rich Dark Chocolate Cake will keep for 3 to 5 days.

VARIATIONS

Change the flavor of this cake by adding other flavoring extracts, such as peppermint or almond. If you can't have chocolate, substitute an equal amount of carob powder; the resulting cake will be just as delicious.

TIP: To make a two-layer cake, double the ingredients and bake the batter using two 9-inch cake pans. This amount of batter can also be used to make a 9 x 13-inch cake. Make a double batch of frosting if you are going to frost these larger cakes.

The use of barley flour in this cake gives it a slightly nutty flavor and makes it suitable for those who suffer from wheat sensitivities. Many carrot cakes rely on a lot of sugar to bring out the flavor of the carrots, but this one contains a generous dose of spices instead and is just lightly sweetened with maple syrup and a little maple sugar.

wheat-free Carrot Nut Cake

YIELD: 9 PIECES

1¾ cups barley flour

4 tablespoons maple sugar

1 teaspoon aluminum-free baking powder

1 teaspoon baking soda

½ teaspoon ground cinnamon

½ teaspoon ground ginger

½ teaspoon ground cloves

½ teaspoon freshly ground nutmeg

⅛ teaspoon sea salt

⅓ cup soymilk or other nondairy milk of choice

⅓ cup filtered water

⅓ cup maple syrup or agave nectar

¼ cup olive oil or safflower oil

1 teaspoon apple cider vinegar

1 teaspoon vanilla extract

1⅓ cups shredded carrots

⅓ cup raisins or currants

⅓ cup finely chopped nuts of choice

Preheat the oven to 350 degrees F. Lightly oil a 9-inch round or square baking pan and set aside. Place the barley flour, 3 tablespoons of the maple sugar, and the baking powder, baking soda, cinnamon, ginger, cloves, nutmeg, and salt in a medium bowl and whisk until well combined. Add the soymilk, water, maple syrup, oil, vinegar, and vanilla extract and whisk until well combined. Add the carrots and raisins to the batter and stir them in with a rubber spatula.

Transfer the batter to the prepared pan. Sprinkle the chopped nuts and remaining 1 tablespoon maple sugar over the top and press them in gently with your hand.

Bake for 30 to 40 minutes or until a toothpick inserted in the center comes out clean. Allow the cake to cool completely before cutting or frosting. Stored in an airtight container at room temperature, Wheat-Free Carrot Nut Cake will keep for 3 to 5 days.

TIP: To make a two-layer cake, double the ingredients and bake the batter using two 9-inch cake pans. This amount of batter can also be used to make a 9 x 13-inch cake. Make a double batch of frosting if you are going to frost these larger cakes.

A humble topping made with rolled oats, turbinado sugar, vanilla, and spices transforms fresh or frozen fruits into a quick and tasty dessert. Apples are most commonly used in fruit crisps, but pears, peaches, nectarines, plums, blueberries, raspberries, strawberries, and even rhubarb, used alone or in combination, also yield delicious results. A scoop of nondairy ice cream or sorbet makes an excellent topping for a serving of warm fruit crisp.

Fruit crisp

YIELD: 3 TO 4 SERVINGS

TOPPING

¾ cup rolled oats

⅓ cup oat flour or barley flour

¼ cup turbinado sugar or other sugar of choice

½ teaspoon ground cinnamon

¼ teaspoon ground ginger or other spice of choice

¼ cup nonhydrogenated margarine

½ teaspoon vanilla extract

FRUIT FILLING

4 to 5 cups fresh or frozen sliced fruit or berries of choice

2 tablespoons oat flour or barley flour

2 to 3 tablespoons turbinado sugar or other sugar of choice

1 teaspoon ground cinnamon or other spice of choice

½ teaspoon ground ginger or other spice of choice

½ teaspoon vanilla extract

Preheat the oven to 375 degrees F. To make the topping, place the oats, oat flour, sugar, cinnamon, and ginger in a small bowl and stir until well combined. Using your fingers, work the margarine and vanilla extract into the dry ingredients until the mixture resembles coarse crumbs.

To make the fruit filling, place all of the fruit filling ingredients in a medium bowl and stir until well combined. Transfer the fruit filling to a 9-inch square baking pan or casserole dish. Sprinkle the topping mixture evenly over the fruit filling.

Bake for 30 to 35 minutes or until golden brown and the filling is bubbly. Allow to cool slightly before serving. Stored in an airtight container in the refrigerator, Fruit Crisp will keep for 3 to 5 days.

VARIATIONS

- For added crunch and nutrition, add ¼ cup chopped nuts or 2 tablespoons sunflower seeds to the topping mixture.
- Add ¼ to ½ cup dried fruit to the fruit filling, such as raisins, currants, or cranberries.

No Oven Required

quick and easy treats

There are many sweet treats and desserts that you can make lovingly with your own two hands without turning on your oven at all, which can come in handy during the hot summer months. Using the stovetop, you can create several sensational sauces for topping pancakes or pieces of cake, for dipping fresh fruit into, or for drizzling on bowlfuls of nondairy ice cream or sorbet. You can also cook up a batch of homemade pudding, a gelled dessert, or a pan of crispy rice cereal treats, which will remind you of the ones you enjoyed as a kid. With the aid of a food processor, you can whip up a tofu-based topping for use on baked goods, or better yet, make a naturally sweetened fruit pie or candies using raw ingredients like dried fruits, nuts, and seeds. Whichever recipe you choose, you're sure to satisfy your cravings for sweets deliciously.

This fruit sauce is flavored and sweetened with a mixture of apple juice and spices rather than sugar, which allows the flavor of the berries to really shine through. Prepare the sauce using any variety of your favorite berries, such as blueberries, blackberries, strawberries, raspberries, or even a combination of mixed berries. Serve it over breakfast items like pancakes, waffles, or French toast, or use it as a topping for desserts, cakes, fresh fruit, or scoops of nondairy ice cream or sorbet.

berry fruit Sauce or Syrup

YIELD: 1½ CUPS

10 ounces fresh or frozen berries of choice
(about 3 to 3½ cups)

⅓ cup apple juice

¼ teaspoon ground cinnamon

⅛ teaspoon ground cardamom

Place all of the ingredients in a small saucepan and bring to a boil over high heat. Reduce the heat to low and simmer for 8 to 10 minutes or until the berries are soft. Remove from the heat and let cool slightly.

For a chunky sauce, place half of the mixture in a blender or food processor and process for 1 to 2 minutes or until completely smooth. Stir the blended mixture into the remaining sauce in the saucepan.

For a syrup, place all of the mixture in a blender or food processor and process for 1 to 2 minutes or until completely smooth.

Serve warm, cold, or at room temperature. Stored in an airtight container in the refrigerator, Berry Fruit Sauce or Syrup will keep for 5 to 7 days.

VARIATIONS

- Substitute other varieties of fresh or frozen fruits, like cherries, peaches, mangoes, or pineapple.
- Replace the ground spices with an equal quantity of other ground spices of your choice, such as ginger, cloves, or nutmeg.

Many people think you can't make a good caramel sauce without using dairy products, but this vegan recipe dispels that myth. A combination of soymilk, turbinado sugar, maple syrup, and vanilla extract is used to create this simple, caramel-flavored sauce. Serve it as a topping for cakes, desserts, or scoops of nondairy ice cream or sorbet, or use it as a dipping sauce for pieces of fresh fruit.

Rich Caramel sauce

YIELD: 1½ CUPS

¾ cup soymilk or other nondairy milk of choice

¾ cup turbinado sugar or other sugar of choice

⅓ cup maple syrup

2 tablespoons cold filtered water

1 tablespoon arrowroot

2 tablespoons nonhydrogenated margarine

1 teaspoon vanilla extract

Place the soymilk, sugar, and maple syrup in a small saucepan and whisk until well combined. Place over medium heat and cook, whisking often, for 3 minutes.

Place the water and arrowroot in a small bowl and stir until dissolved. Whisk the mixture into the saucepan and cook, whisking often, for 2 to 3 minutes or until thickened.

Remove from the heat. Whisk in the margarine and vanilla extract. Serve warm, cold, or at room temperature. Stored in an airtight container in the refrigerator, Rich Caramel Sauce will keep for 5 to 7 days.

This hot fudge sauce is so rich and chocolaty that you will be tempted to eat it with a spoon. Serve it as a topping for cakes, desserts, or scoops of nondairy ice cream or sorbet, or use it as a dipping sauce for pieces of fresh fruit.

Hot Fudge sauce

YIELD: 1½ CUPS

⅔ cup cocoa powder

2 tablespoons cornstarch

1⅓ cups soymilk or other nondairy milk of choice

⅓ cup agave nectar

1 teaspoon vanilla extract

Place the cocoa powder and cornstarch in a small saucepan and whisk well to remove any lumps. Add the soymilk and agave nectar and cook over medium heat, whisking often, for 2 to 3 minutes or until thickened.

Remove from the heat and whisk in the vanilla extract. Serve warm or at room temperature. Stored in an airtight container in the refrigerator, Hot Fudge Sauce will keep for 5 to 7 days.

VARIATIONS

- Add additional flavoring extracts, such as peppermint, orange, or almond.
- If you are unable to have chocolate, substitute an equal amount of carob powder to make a carob-flavored fudge sauce.

Most of us have fond memories of sucking on ice pops during the hot summer months, and it is very easy to make your own homemade versions of these frozen treats. Nowadays, you can purchase ice pop molds in various shapes and sizes at most retail stores. With a few additions and very little effort, you can transform a container of soy yogurt into delicately sweet and decadent frozen ice pops or custard.

frozen Yogurt Berry Pops

YIELD: 4 SERVINGS

6 ounces vanilla soy yogurt

3 tablespoons fresh or frozen blueberries

2 tablespoons agave nectar

1 teaspoon freshly squeezed lemon juice

1 teaspoon vanilla extract

Place all of the ingredients in a small bowl and stir until well combined. Alternatively, for a smoother texture, mash the blueberries in the bowl first and then add all of the remaining ingredients.

Pour the mixture into 4 three-ounce ice pop molds, dividing it evenly among the molds. Insert the mold sticks and freeze for at least 8 to 12 hours or until the pops are frozen solid.

For easy removal from the molds, allow the frozen pops to sit at room temperature for several minutes or dip the molds quickly in hot water. Serve immediately. Stored in their molds in the freezer, Frozen Yogurt Berry Pops will keep for 1 month.

VARIATIONS

To create additional ice pop flavors, substitute other flavors of soy yogurt, different types of fresh or frozen berries or chopped fruit, and/or other citrus fruit juices.

TIPS

- Mini paper cups and wooden sticks or spoons can be used instead of the ice pop molds.
- If you prefer, pour the mixture into ice cube trays and freeze until solid. Serve several frozen cubes in a bowl and eat them with a spoon, like frozen custard.

Drying fruits concentrates and preserves their flavors. Because dried fruits are tasty and convenient, they are great to have on hand to satisfy a sweet tooth. In this recipe, a variety of dried fruits are blended together to create delectable, raw, coconut-covered treats, which you can enjoy whenever you crave something sweet.

dried Fruit, Nut, and Coconut candies

YIELD: 8 TO 9 PIECES

½ cup dried apricots

½ cup pitted dates

½ cup raw nuts or seeds of choice

⅓ cup raisins

¼ teaspoon ground ginger

½ cup unsweetened shredded dried coconut, plus 3 to 4 tablespoons for coating

1 tablespoon freshly squeezed orange juice

Zest of ½ medium orange (1 to 2 tablespoons)

Place the apricots, dates, nuts, raisins, and ginger in a food processor and process for 1 to 2 minutes or until finely ground. Add the ½ cup coconut, orange juice, and half of the orange zest and process for 1 to 2 minutes or until the mixture comes together to form a ball.

Place the 3 to 4 tablespoons coconut on a small plate. Add the remaining orange zest and gently toss until well combined.

Dampen your hands with water. Form the blended mixture into 1-inch balls. Roll the balls in the shredded coconut mixture until they are evenly coated on all sides. Serve immediately. Stored in an airtight container, leftover Dried Fruit, Nut, and Coconut Candies will keep for 7 days in the refrigerator or for 3 months in the freezer.

VARIATIONS

For alternate flavors, substitute an equal amount of other varieties of dried fruits.

Energize your mind, body, and spirit by snacking on a few of these treats shaped like mini candy bars. Made with wholesome raw ingredients, they will naturally satisfy your cravings for sweets. This delightful combination of dried fruits, nuts, and seeds will also supply you with an assortment of vitamins, minerals, antioxidants, and essential fatty acids. Take them along when you go hiking or traveling, or enjoy them as part of a nutritious grab-and-go breakfast when paired with a smoothie.

Mother Nature's candy bars

YIELD: 8 PIECES

2 tablespoons flaxseeds

2 tablespoons filtered water

2 tablespoons raw hemp seeds

2 tablespoons raw pumpkin seeds

2 tablespoons raw sunflower seeds

½ teaspoon ground cinnamon

¼ cup dried cherries

¼ cup raw nuts of choice

2 dried figs of choice

Place the flaxseeds in a food processor and process for 30 seconds or until finely ground. Transfer to a small bowl. Add the water and set aside for 10 minutes.

Place the hemp seeds, pumpkin seeds, sunflower seeds, and cinnamon in the food processor (there's no need to wash it first) and process for 30 seconds or until finely ground. Transfer 3 tablespoons of this mixture to a small plate and set aside.

Add the flaxseed mixture and the cherries, nuts, and figs to the food processor and process for 1 to 2 minutes or until the mixture comes together to form a ball.

Dampen your hands with water and form the mixture into 3-inch bars. Roll the bars in the reserved seed mixture until the bars are evenly coated on all sides. Serve immediately. Stored in an airtight container, leftover Mother Nature's Candy Bards will keep for 7 days in the refrigerator or for 3 months in the freezer.

VARIATIONS

For alternate flavors, substitute an equal amount of other varieties of dried fruits, nuts, and/or seeds.

Most store-bought pies are made with refined ingredients like flour, sugar, and fat, but this naturally sweetened, uncooked pie is made with only healthful raw ingredients. You can even eat a piece of this sweet, nutritious pie for breakfast without any guilt! Express your artistic side by decoratively garnishing your pie with a selection of sliced fresh fruits or berries and a few handfuls of sliced almonds and shredded coconut.

raw Fruity Goodness Pie

YIELD: 8 PIECES

CRUST

½ cup raw almonds

½ cup raw walnuts

½ cup raw sunflower seeds

½ cup unsweetened dried banana chips

1½ cups pitted dates

½ teaspoon ground cinnamon

FRUIT FILLING

2 cups blueberries

1½ cups sliced strawberries

¼ cup pitted dates

½ teaspoon ground cinnamon

Toppings of choice, such as sliced fresh fruits or berries, sliced almonds, and/or unsweetened shredded dried coconut

To make the crust, place the almonds, walnuts, sunflower seeds, and banana chips in a food processor and process for 1 to 2 minutes or until finely ground. Add the dates and cinnamon and process for 2 to 3 minutes or until the mixture comes together to form a ball.

To form the crust, using your hands, press the mixture firmly and evenly into the bottom and up the sides of a 9-inch glass pie pan. Chill the crust in the refrigerator for 20 to 30 minutes or until firm to the touch.

To make the fruit filling, wipe out the food processor with a clean towel. Place the blueberries, strawberries, dates, and cinnamon in the food processor and process for 1 to 2 minutes. Scrape down the sides of the container and process for 1 minute longer or until completely smooth.

Remove the crust from the refrigerator and pour the filling into it. Chill the pie in the refrigerator for at least 30 to 45 minutes or until the filling is set and slightly firm to the touch.

Cut the pie into 8 pieces. Decorate each piece with your choice of toppings. Serve immediately. Stored covered with plastic wrap in the refrigerator, leftover Raw Fruity Goodness Pie will keep for 2 to 3 days.

Boxed gelatins come in a variety of rainbow colors and flavors and are promoted as a healthful dessert. But these products really aren't nutritious, as they often contain artificial flavorings and sweeteners, and, of course, gelatin itself is made from the connective tissue of animals—a rather unsavory concept! In this recipe, fruit juices and fresh strawberries provide all of the necessary coloring and sweetness, and agar, a sea vegetable, is used as the gelling agent.

gelled Fruity Dessert

YIELD: 2 TO 3 SERVINGS

1 cup red raspberry juice or other fruit juice of choice (see tip)

1 tablespoon agar flakes, or 1½ teaspoons agar powder

½ teaspoon vanilla extract

1 cup sliced strawberries or other fruit or berries of choice (see tip)

Place the juice and agar flakes in a small saucepan and bring to a boil over high heat. Reduce the heat to low and cook, stirring often, for 5 to 10 minutes or until the agar is thoroughly dissolved.

Remove from the heat and stir in the vanilla extract. Set aside for 10 minutes to cool slightly. Pour the mixture into a medium glass bowl and chill it in the refrigerator for 30 minutes or until partially set.

Gently stir in the sliced strawberries and chill the mixture for several hours longer or until it has gelled completely and is slightly firm to the touch. Stored covered with plastic wrap or in an airtight container in the refrigerator, Gelled Fruity Dessert will keep for 3 to 5 days.

TIP: Citrus fruits and pineapple do not react well with agar and may cause gelling problems. Either omit them or use them in combination with other varieties of fruit or fruit juices for the proper results.

There is no need to open a box to make pudding when you can whip up a batch from scratch, the old-fashioned way, in no time. Enjoy this pudding plain or topped with a dollop of Whipped Tofu Topping (page 133), sliced fresh fruit or berries, chopped vegan chocolate or nuts, or toasted shredded coconut. It also makes a terrific no-bake pie filling.

old-fashioned Vanilla Pudding and pie filling

YIELD: 3 TO 4 SERVINGS

2 cups soymilk or other nondairy milk of choice

¼ cup unbleached cane sugar or beet sugar

2 tablespoons cornstarch

1 teaspoon vanilla extract

Place the soymilk, sugar, and cornstarch in a small saucepan and cook over medium heat, whisking often, for 2 to 3 minutes or until thickened. Remove the saucepan from the heat and whisk in the vanilla extract.

Pour into a medium glass bowl or small individual serving bowls. Cover with parchment paper or plastic wrap to prevent a skin from forming. Chill in the refrigerator for 1 hour or longer before serving. Stored covered with plastic wrap or in an airtight container in the refrigerator, Old-Fashioned Vanilla Pudding and Pie Filling will keep for 3 to 5 days.

VARIATIONS

- Add other flavorings extracts to the pudding, such as almond, lemon, peppermint, coconut, or maple.
- Whisk a few tablespoons of cocoa or carob powder into the mixture prior to heating.
- To use the pudding as a pie filling, fill a prebaked pie crust or graham cracker crust with the warm mixture. Chill the pie in the refrigerator for several hours or until slightly firm to the touch. Garnish individual slices or decorate the pie as desired before cutting.

TIP: Portion the chilled pudding into individual airtight containers for traveling.

This delicious and versatile dairy-free replacement for whipped cream comes together in minutes. You can sweeten it with your choice of unbleached cane sugar, maple syrup, or agave nectar. Serve it as a topping for fresh fruit or berries, granola, pies, cakes, and desserts, or enjoy all on its own.

whipped Tofu Topping

YIELD: 1½ CUPS

1 package (12 ounces) **firm or extra-firm silken tofu**

¼ to ⅓ cup **sweetener of choice**

2 teaspoons **safflower oil**

1½ teaspoons **vanilla extract**

Place all of the ingredients in a food processor and process for 1 minute. Scrape down the sides of the container and process for 1 to 2 minutes longer or until completely smooth and light and creamy.

Transfer to a small bowl, cover, and chill in the refrigerator for 1 hour or longer. Stored covered with plastic wrap or in an airtight container in the refrigerator, Whipped Tofu Topping will keep for 3 to 5 days.

VARIATIONS

Add other flavorings extracts, such as almond or peppermint, or a little fruit juice and/or citrus zest, such as lemon, lime, or orange.

Treats made with crispy rice cereal are a popular childhood favorite, but they are abandoned by vegans because they're typically made with marshmallows, which contain gelatin, and butter. In this delicious vegan version, a creamy mixture of nut butter and brown rice syrup is used instead of animal products to flavor and bind the rice cereal.

crispy Rice Cereal Treats

YIELD: 9 SQUARES

½ cup unsweetened shredded dried coconut

2 cups crispy brown rice cereal

½ cup chopped nuts of choice

½ cup brown rice syrup

½ cup nut butter of choice

1 teaspoon vanilla extract

¼ teaspoon sea salt

½ cup vegan chocolate or carob chips

Lightly oil a 9-inch square baking pan and set aside. Place the coconut in a small skillet and toast it over low heat, stirring often, for 2 to 3 minutes or until lightly colored. Transfer to a medium bowl. Add the cereal and nuts and stir until well combined.

Place the brown rice syrup and nut butter in the same skillet and warm over low heat, stirring often, for 1 to 2 minutes or until thoroughly heated and small bubbles begin to appear around the edges.

Remove from the heat and stir in the vanilla extract and salt. Pour over the cereal mixture and stir gently but thoroughly until evenly coated. Stir in the chocolate chips.

Transfer the mixture to the prepared pan. Dampen your hands with water and press the mixture firmly and evenly into the pan. Chill in the refrigerator for 30 minutes or until firm to the touch.

Using a metal spatula or knife, loosen the chilled mixture from the sides of the pan and cut it into 9 squares. Stored in an airtight container at room temperature, Crispy Rice Cereal Treats will keep for 3 to 5 days.

GLOSSARY

Special Ingredients

You can purchase these items in most supermarkets and natural food stores as well as many ethnic and gourmet specialty markets. They are available in bulk or prepackaged containers of various sizes.

Agar. Agar, also known as agar-agar and kanten, is an odorless and tasteless gelatinous substance derived from seaweed. It is commonly used as a binder, thickening agent, and replacement for animal-based gelatin in recipes. Agar can be purchased as sticks, flakes, or powder.

Agave nectar. Agave nectar, also known as agave syrup, is extracted from agave cactus plants, which are native to central Mexico. Raw agave nectar is rich in naturally occurring enzymes, metabolizes slowly, and can be used measure for measure as a replacement for honey or maple syrup in most recipes. It's available in both light and amber-colored varieties. Stored at room temperature or in the refrigerator, agave nectar will keep for up to a year.

Aluminum-free baking powder. Aluminum-free baking powder is made without aluminum-based salts. Aluminum ingestion has been linked to Alzheimer's disease and other health problems. This type of baking powder is well-suited for vegan baking because it is double-acting, which means it reacts in two stages: once when subjected to moisture during mixing, and again when subjected to heat in the oven.

Arrowroot. Arrowroot is a starch obtained from the rhizomes, or tubers, of various tropical plants. Historically it was used to heal arrow wounds, hence the name. It's used as a binder and thickening agent and as a partial replacement for wheat flour in gluten-free baking. Arrowroot is absolutely tasteless and becomes clear when cooked. Unlike cornstarch, it doesn't impart a chalky taste when undercooked. It should be dissolved in cold water or other cold liquid before being heated or added to hot mixtures.

Balsamic vinegar. Balsamic vinegar is traditionally manufactured in Modena, Italy, from the concentrated juice of white Trebbiano grapes. It is dark brown and very aromatic, with a rich, sweet, and complex flavor. Balsamic vinegar is known for being aged in a successive number of casks made of various types of wood, which are used to develop the flavor of the final product. Most balsamic vinegar is aged for three to twelve years; the longer it's aged, the higher the price.

Barley flour. Barley flour is made by finely grinding hulled or pearled barley. It adds subtle, nutty flavor and healthful fiber to baked goods and can be used to replace all or part of the amount of wheat flour needed in recipes. Barley flour is often paired with oat flour or spelt flour in wheat-free baking.

Beet sugar. Beet sugar is made from sugar beets, a variety of beets that is off-white in color and has a high sugar content. Unlike cane sugar, beet sugar is naturally white and is never processed with bone char (a bleaching agent); thus it is suitable for vegans. Beet sugar can be used measure for measure as a replacement for cane sugar in recipes, including the ones in this book.

Brown rice syrup. Brown rice syrup is a liquid sweetener made by fermenting brown rice with special enzymes until its natural starches begin to break down. The mixture is then strained and cooked down to a syrupy consistency. Brown rice syrup has a mildly sweet and light caramel flavor and color, with a consistency similar to honey but with half the sweetness of honey or sugar. It's available gluten free and in several flavored varieties. Stored tightly covered in a cool, dry place or in the refrigerator, brown rice syrup will keep for up to a year.

Brown rice vinegar. Brown rice vinegar is made from fermented brown rice, water, and koji (a beneficial type of mold), or from unrefined rice wine (sake) and water (also known as seasoned brown rice vinegar); it is then aged in wooden barrels or crocks. Both varieties of brown rice vinegar have a mellow, slightly sweet flavor, are golden or amber in color, and have a low to moderate acid content. Either one can be used for preparing the recipes in this book.

Bulgur. Bulgur is made from wheat berries that have been washed, steamed or parboiled, dried, and then crushed or cracked into small, coarse pieces. Bulgur is often confused with cracked wheat, which is wheat that has been cracked into small pieces but not parboiled or steamed. Bulgur has a nutty flavor and chewy texture and requires little time or effort to prepare.

Capers. Capers are the edible, immature flower buds of a shrub that grows wild on walls or in rocky coastal areas throughout the Mediterranean. The small, dark green capers are commonly pickled in a vinegar-based solution. Capers have a sharp, distinct flavor, and only a small amount of them is needed in recipes. Once opened, a jar of capers should be stored in the refrigerator where it will keep for 6 to 8 months.

Carob powder. Carob powder is made by grinding the dried pulp from the pods of the carob tree, an evergreen native to the Mediterranean. Carob is also known as locust bean and St. John's Bread (in reference to John the Baptist). The large, sweet-tasting carob pods have been used as food for animals and humans since prehistoric times. Carob powder is available raw or roasted and is often used measure for measure as a substitute for cocoa powder, but unlike cocoa, it's caffeine free.

Cornstarch. Cornstarch is a white, powdery starch obtained from corn. Cornstarch is used as a binder and thickening agent in recipes and also as an anticaking agent in the production of powdered sugar. It should be dissolved in cold water or other cool liquid before being heated or added to hot mixtures. Cornstarch has a slightly chalky taste.

Couscous. Couscous is actually a type of pasta, but due to its small size, it is often referred to as a grain. Couscous is made by rolling semolina wheat flour and a little water into very small pellets. At one time it was extremely labor-intensive to make and prepare couscous. Fortunately for modern cooks, a quick-cooking variety was developed, and this is the type that you will find readily available.

Cremini mushrooms. Cremini mushrooms, also known as baby bellas and brown mushrooms, are the slightly more flavorful cousins of the common white button mushrooms. Large cremini mushrooms are called portobello mushrooms. Cremini mushrooms can be eaten raw or cooked and may be substituted for button mushrooms in any recipe.

Crispy brown rice cereal. Crispy brown rice cereal is made from oven-toasted brown rice that has been lightly sweetened with gluten-free brown rice syrup or barley malt. It can be enjoyed as a breakfast cereal and also used to make snack mixes and Crispy Rice Cereal Treats (page 134).

Dijon mustard. Dijon mustard is made from husked brown or black mustard seeds, which are blended with wine or verjuice (an acidic, sour liquid made from unripe grapes) and other ingredients. The original method of preparation originated in Dijon, France, hence the name. It has a pale yellow color and its flavor varies from mildly spicy to very hot. Dijon mustard is commonly used as a condiment and ingredient to flavor recipes.

Flaxseeds. Flaxseeds are the small, edible seeds harvested from the flax plant, also known as linseed. They have a slightly nutty flavor; are high in fiber, protein, and omega-3 essential fatty acids; and are rich in vitamins, minerals, and lignans (an important antioxidant and phytoestrogen). When combined with liquids, flaxseeds will turn into a gummy, gel-like substance, so they're often used as a binder and egg replacement in baking. To make a replacement for 1 egg, mix 1 tablespoon whole or ground flaxseeds with 3 tablespoons water, and set aside for several minutes or until the mixture thickens and becomes gelatinous. Flaxseeds come in two colors, brown and golden, and are available whole or ground, which is also known as flaxseed meal. Stored in an airtight container in a cool, dry place or in the refrigerator or freezer, flaxseeds will keep for 6 to 8 months.

Flaxseed oil. Flaxseed oil is a cold expeller-pressed oil obtained from flaxseeds. Flaxseed oil is quite nutritious, with a slightly nutty flavor and a dark brown color. It is sold in dark-colored containers because its nutrients are easily destroyed by heat, light, and oxygen. For this reason, never use flaxseed oil for cooking; instead, use it in salad dressings or add it to foods after cooking, just before serving. Stored in the refrigerator, flaxseed oil will keep for 6 to 8 months.

Garnet yams. Garnet yams are long, sweet-tasting tubers that have deep red skins (some have a slight purple tinge to them) and orange-colored flesh. They are often considered the most flavorful variety of yams. What is commonly sold in the United States as a "yam" is actually a sweet potato. However, the two tubers are quite different in flavor and appearance; sweet potatoes are much moister and sweeter, and they have a less starchy texture compared to the true yams, cultivated in other parts of the world. If you cannot find garnet yams, substitute with Beauregard yams, jewel yams, or what are simply labeled generically as sweet potatoes.

Gold beets. Gold beets have an orange exterior and a deep yellow-gold interior instead of the more common red color that we typically associate with beets. Their mild, slightly sweet flavor makes them suitable for use in both raw and cooked dishes. Gold beets don't bleed like the red ones often do when they are added to dishes, but they can darken when they are peeled and exposed to air. Rinsing them before and after peeling will inhibit this natural discoloration.

Hemp seeds. Hemp seeds are small, edible seeds harvested from the versatile hemp plant. Also called hemp nuts, these nutritious seeds are sterilized to prevent germination and shelled prior to sale. Hemp seeds have a nutty flavor similar to pine nuts or sunflower seeds and are rich in essential amino acids, vitamins, minerals, and fiber. They also are among the most balanced sources of omega-3 and omega-6 essential fatty acids (EFAs). Hemp seeds are often eaten raw as a snack, added to recipes, ground into flour, and processed to make nondairy milk, cheese, ice cream, margarine, and oil. Stored in an airtight container in a cool, dry place or in the refrigerator or freezer, hemp seeds will keep for 6 to 8 months.

Hemp seed oil. Hemp seed oil is a cold expeller-pressed oil obtained from hemp seeds. It has a slightly nutty odor and bright green color (due to its high chlorophyll content) and can be used much like flaxseed oil in recipes. It is sold in dark-colored containers because its nutrients are easily destroyed by heat, light, and oxygen. For this reason, hemp seed oil is not recommended for frying; if you must heat it, do so gently and only for a short period of time. Stored in the refrigerator, hemp seed oil will keep for 6 to 8 months.

Horseradish, prepared. Prepared horseradish is made with the freshly grated root of the horseradish plant and a seasoned vinegar solution. It's white to creamy beige in color and has a spicy to hot, pungent flavor. Prepared horseradish is commonly used as a flavoring or condiment, and when combined with ketchup, it's called cocktail sauce. Once opened, prepared horseradish will keep for several months in the refrigerator, but eventually it will start to darken, indicating it is losing flavor and should be replaced.

Italian seasoning blend. Italian seasoning blend is a mixture of dried herbs that are commonly used in Italian cuisine, such as basil, oregano, marjoram, thyme, rosemary, and sage. If you can't find it in your area, substitute an equal amount of dried basil and oregano.

Lite coconut milk. Lite coconut milk is a thinner, lighter version of regular coconut milk, with typically 70 percent less fat than regular coconut milk. Lite coconut milk can be used as a replacement for regular coconut milk in most recipes.

Maple sugar. Maple sugar is made from evaporated maple syrup and was first produced, used, and distributed by Native Americans. It has a very sweet, almost nutty flavor. Maple sugar can be used as a replacement for cane sugar or other granulated sweeteners in recipes, but use a lesser amount because it has twice the sweetness of cane sugar. It is available as a powder, granules, or crystals. Use either crystals or granules for preparing the recipes in this book.

Millet. Millet belongs to a group of several small-seeded species of grains or cereal crops that are widely grown throughout the world. It's rich in fiber, protein, vitamins, and minerals. Millet has a mildly sweet, nutty flavor and is commonly used as a grain or ground into flour for gluten-free baking.

Miso. Miso is a thick paste made by fermenting soybeans and/or other beans and grains, such as rice or barley, along with salt and koji (a beneficial type of mold). It's a very nutritious and versatile ingredient that is often used as a condiment or seasoning to add flavor to recipes. Depending on the type, miso imparts a delicate or strong flavor, which is often described as sweet, savory, or salty. White, mellow, chickpea, and barley miso create a light flavor and color, while red or *hatcho* miso will result in a deeper, stronger, and more robust flavor and color. Stored tightly covered in the refrigerator, miso will keep for several months.

Mixed grain blends. Mixed grain blends are produced by several companies and often contain assorted varieties of rice, wild rice, and/or other grains. Some may also include seeds, seasonings, or dehydrated vegetables. Using mixed grain blends is an easy and affordable way to incorporate more types of grains into your daily diet.

Nondairy milks. Nondairy milks are creamy beverages or liquids made with plant-based ingredients. They can be used measure for measure as a replacement for cow's milk in most recipes without affecting the finished product. Commonly found nondairy milks include soymilk, rice milk, coconut milk, almond milk, hazelnut milk, oat milk, multigrain milk, and hemp milk. Many are available in assorted flavors as well. Nondairy milks do vary in flavor and consistency from manufacturer to manufacturer, so taste and compare them to determine which brands suit your tastes. They are found in the refrigerated section or on shelves in aseptic cartons.

Nonhydrogenated margarine. Nonhydrogenated margarine is made with a combination of cold expeller-pressed oils and can be used measure for measure as a replacement for butter or other margarine in most recipes. Nonhydrogenated margarine does not contain trans fats, which are harmful, man-made fats that can raise blood cholesterol levels, clog arteries, and lead to weight gain and even heart disease. It is available in tubs in both ready-to-spread regular and whipped varieties; it is also packaged in sticks. Stored in its original packaging in the refrigerator, nonhydrogenated margarine will keep for several months.

Nut butters. Nut butters are made from either raw or roasted nuts that are ground into a smooth or chunky paste. Peanut butter is the most commonly recognized nut butter, but others that are also delicious include almond, cashew, hazelnut, pecan, and soy nut butters. You can purchase nut butters in jars or from dispensers where you can freshly grind them yourself. Due to their high oil content, nut butters may separate during storage. Just stir the oil back in before you use them. Refrigeration will minimize this separation, and because nut butters can become rancid quickly, refrigerating them will also help them keep longer.

Nutritional yeast. Nutritional yeast is made from a deactivated form of yeast grown on a molasses medium and is a cousin to the live yeasts used for leavening (baker's yeast) and fermenting (brewer's yeast). Red Star Vegetarian Support Formula nutritional yeast is the most widely available brand of nutritional yeast in the United States and is suitable for vegans; other nutritional yeast brands may contain animal-based products, so check the product labels. Nutritional yeast has a remarkable cheeselike and somewhat nutty flavor, so it's often used to season nondairy cheese products and other foods. It's also a delicious, convenient vegan source of amino acids, important minerals, folic acid, and vitamin B_{12}. It is available in flakes or a fine powder. The flakes are preferred for the recipes in this book because they have more texture. If only the powder is available, use half the amount called for in the recipe.

Pine nuts. Pine nuts, also known as pignolia, pignoli, or piñon, are the edible seeds found inside pine cones of certain species of pine trees. Toasting pine nuts briefly in a dry skillet or in the oven until lightly browned and fragrant heightens their flavor, but they're also delicious raw as a snack or added to recipes.

Portobello mushrooms. Portobello mushrooms are actually large-sized cremini mushrooms. They have a rich, earthy flavor and aroma, and a large, open, flat cap, which can be cut into thick slices for use in recipes. The caps are also often left whole and marinated, cooked, and served as meatless burger patties.

Quinoa. Quinoa is a small, quick-cooking grain, first used by the Aztecs and Incas, that comes in a wide variety of colors, including yellow, red, purple, and black. It is considered a "supergrain" because it contains all of the essential amino acids, fiber, and many vitamins and minerals, including calcium (one cup of quinoa contains more absorbable calcium than a quart of cow's milk).

Quinoa is naturally covered with a bitter-tasting coating called saponin. Most quinoa sold today has been prerinsed, which removes this coating, but it's still recommended that you rinse quinoa in a fine-mesh strainer prior to cooking, just to be on the safe side.

Red wine vinegar. Red wine vinegar is made from fermented red wine and tends to have less acidity than white or cider vinegars. As with wine, there is a considerable range in quality between various brands of red wine vinegar (the variety of grapes used and the length of aging affect its final flavor), so taste and compare to determine which brands suit your tastes.

Safflower oil. Safflower oil is cold expeller-pressed oil made from the seeds of the safflower plant, which is also called saffron thistle. Safflower oil has a mild flavor, so it works well in baked goods and is commonly used as cooking oil, especially for deep-frying, due to its high smoke point. It contains more polyunsaturated fat than any other oil and is often used in margarines and bottled salad dressings. Stored in the pantry or in the refrigerator, safflower oil will keep for up to a year.

Seitan. Seitan is often called gluten or wheat meat because it's made from the concentrated gluten protein found in wheat. Its texture is often described as spongy, firm, chewy, or meatlike, so it's commonly used as a replacement for beef, chicken, and pork in vegetarian and vegan dishes and in the production of vegan meat analogs. Seitan can be made by hand, the traditional way, by continuously rinsing whole wheat flour with water to remove the starch, or by a faster method using vital wheat gluten (also called instant gluten flour), after which it's usually simmered in broth or baked. You can also purchase prepackaged seitan in blocks, chunks, pieces, or strips in assorted flavors. It is often covered with a tasty liquid or sauce. To save time, use prepackaged seitan for preparing the recipes in this book.

Shiitake mushrooms. Shiitake mushrooms have brown, slightly convex caps, which range in size from two to four inches in diameter, and, like all varieties of mushrooms, have a chewy, meaty flesh. Shiitake mushrooms can be eaten raw or cooked, and are available fresh or dried. Only fresh shiitakes are used for preparing the recipes in this book.

Soy yogurt. Soy yogurt is made by fermenting soymilk with live cultures (such as *L. acidophilus* and *B. bifidum*), often referred to as friendly bacteria, in a process similar to the production of dairy yogurt. Soy yogurt can be eaten or used in recipes just like dairy yogurt. It is available in assorted flavors, with or without fruit added.

Spelt flour. Spelt flour is made from finely ground spelt berries, an ancient grain that is similar in appearance to wheat berries but is an entirely different species. Spelt flour is commonly used in wheat-free baking and is available in both whole grain and white flour varieties. Whole grain spelt flour is recommended for preparing the recipes in this book.

Sun-dried tomato pieces. Sun-dried tomato pieces are made from ripe tomatoes that have been left to dry in the sun to remove their natural water content. They are sold in halves, pieces, or strips and used to add flavor and color to dishes. If you can only find them sold as halves, simply cut them into small pieces using scissors or a sharp knife.

Tahini. Tahini is a smooth paste made from ground sesame seeds; its appearance and texture are similar to peanut butter. Due to its high oil content, tahini may separate and need to be stirred before it is used. Storing tahini in the refrigerator will help keep the oil from separating out again and will also prevent it from going rancid.

Tamari. Tamari is a dark and rich-flavored Japanese soy sauce made from fermented miso or a mixture of water, soybeans, salt, and koji (a beneficial type of mold). It is usually aged for two years in wooden barrels or metal tanks. Tamari is also wheat and gluten free. Tamari and other naturally brewed sauces should always be kept out of direct light or stored in the refrigerator; it will keep for up to a year.

Tempeh. Tempeh is made from soybeans, alone or in combination with other beans or grains, such as barley, rice, millet, quinoa, or lentils. The ingredients are injected with a special mold culture and left to ferment, which causes them to bind together and form a thick slab with edible veins running through it ranging in color from white, brown, and gray to black. As a result of the fermentation process, tempeh is more digestible than tofu; and it also has a richer flavor similar to mushrooms, so it's often used as a replacement for beef in recipes.

Toasted sesame oil. Toasted sesame oil is made from toasted and pressed sesame seeds. It's very aromatic, with a slightly thick consistency and a dark amber-brown color. Toasted sesame oil can burn easily, so it's usually added during the final stages of stir-frying or cooking, but it can be used in dishes that are oven baked with very little problem. Stored in a cool, dark place, toasted sesame oil will keep for several months.

Tofu, regular (firm or extra-firm). Firm or extra-firm regular tofu, also known as bean curd, is a soy-based, cheeselike block made in a process similar to the production of dairy cheese. This tofu is made by coagulating soymilk, which causes it to curdle, and separating the curds (solids) from the whey (liquid). It is then packed in molds, pressed, and left to drain to the desired consistency and texture. Depending on the final texture, the tofu is labeled as soft, firm, or extra-firm. Use either firm or extra-firm to prepare the savory recipes that appear in this book. Regular tofu can be found in water-packed containers in the refrigerated section of your supermarket or natural food store. Tofu should always be stored in the refrigerator. Once you have opened the package, store any remaining tofu covered with water in an airtight container in the refrigerator and change the water daily; stored in this fashion, regular tofu will keep for 3 to 5 days.

Tofu, silken. Silken tofu is a soy-based, cheeselike block that has a smooth, creamy, custardlike texture. It is often blended for use in recipes. Unlike regular tofu, the curds and whey of silken tofu are not separated and some brands actually pour the soymilk and coagulant directly into the packaging and leave the mixture to firm up on its own. Depending on the final texture, the tofu is labeled as soft, firm, or extra-firm. Use either firm or extra-firm silken tofu for preparing the dessert recipes in this book. Silken tofu is available in water-packed containers in the refrigerated section of your supermarket or natural food store, or in aseptic containers on the shelves. Once you have opened the package, store any remaining tofu covered with water in an airtight container in the refrigerator and change the water daily. Stored in this fashion, silken tofu will keep for 3 to 5 days.

Turbinado sugar. Turbinado sugar is made by steaming unrefined raw sugar to create a sugarcane extract, which is then spun in a cylinder or turbine, thus the name. It has a dark brown color and a subtle molasses flavor, with a small, almost crystalline and slightly crunchy texture, so it often used as a replacement for brown sugar in recipes and to decorate the tops of baked goods and beverages.

Unbleached. cane sugar. Unbleached cane sugar is made from sugarcane. Its juice is extracted, any impurities are removed, and then it's evaporated, dried, and crystallized. It's processed without the use of bone char (a bleaching agent), so it's suitable for vegans, and can be used measure for measure as a replacement for white sugar in recipes. You may also see it referred to as unbleached, evaporated sugarcane juice crystals, evaporated cane juice, evaporated cane juice sugar, dehydrated cane juice, or other variations of these names.

Unsweetened dried banana chips. Unsweetened dried banana chips are made by dehydrating slices of fully ripened bananas without any added sweetener or coating. They should not be confused with sweetened banana chips, which are typically coated with sugar or honey and then oven baked or deep-fried. Unsweetened dried banana chips have a naturally sweet, intense banana flavor and a light, crisp, and crunchy texture.

Vegan Parmesan. Vegan Parmesan has a remarkable cheeselike flavor and is a nondairy alternative to dairy-based Parmesan and Pecorino Romano cheeses. It's available in both a soy-based version and a raw version made from walnuts, nutritional yeast, and sea salt. Both varieties can be used to season and flavor foods and in recipes.

Vegan powdered sugar. Vegan powdered sugar is made from vegan-suitable cane sugar or beet sugar that is processed with cornstarch or other starches to prevent caking. Several companies sell vegan powdered sugar, often stating "vegan" right on the package label; a few of them are also organic.

Whole grain bread products. Whole grain bread products are made from whole grains and whole grain flours, which means that they haven't been overly processed or refined and still have their natural bran, germ, and endosperm intact. Check food product labels and look for words such as "wholemeal" or "whole wheat" (or other whole grain varieties) and avoid products with words such as "enriched" or "bromated" on their labels. Whole grain bread products are commonly made from wheat, brown rice, oats, barley, corn, millet, and spelt. Also available are bread products that contain no flour at all; they are often labeled as sprouted grain bread. These products are commonly made with a combination of sprouted grains, beans, and seeds. Whole grain bread products can easily become rancid and are best stored in the refrigerator or freezer.

Whole grain mustard. Whole grain mustard has a grainy texture instead of being smooth like other prepared mustards. That's because it's made with whole or partially ground mustard seeds, which are suspended within the other mustard ingredients. They are available in a variety of styles and flavors, so taste and compare them to determine which brands best suit your needs. Whole grain mustard is commonly used as a condiment and to add flavor to recipes.

Whole grain pasta. Whole grain pasta is pasta made with whole grains, such as wheat, brown rice, corn, quinoa, and even sprouted grains. It is more nutritious than the highly refined varieties that are made with white, enriched, or semolina flour. Whole grain pastas often take a few additional minutes to cook (check the package for exact cooking times) and have a slightly chewier consistency, but they are often lower in calories and more easily digested. You can purchase whole grain pastas in all of your favorite shapes, sizes, flavors, and colors.

Whole wheat pastry flour. Whole wheat pastry flour is made by finely grinding soft white wheat (a specific strain of wheat). It has a lower protein and gluten content than ordinary whole wheat flour, which makes it the preferred choice for pastries, cakes, and other baked goods.

Zest. Zest is the colorful outer skin of citrus fruit. It's commonly used to add extra flavor to recipes, especially desserts and baked goods, without adding extra moisture. Use a zester, vegetable peeler, or paring knife to remove the colored part of the peel only, avoiding the white membrane layer underneath (known as the pith) because it's bitter tasting. Be sure to use the zest from organic citrus fruits only to avoid ingesting any pesticide residues. Store extra zest in an airtight container in the freezer; it will keep for several months and can be added to foods and baked goods without being thawed.

AUTHOR

About the Author

Beverly Lynn Bennett is an organic vegan chef, writer, and animal lover who lives and works in Eugene, Oregon. A chef for over twenty years, she has spent the past twelve years working for various vegan and vegetarian restaurants and natural food stores in both Ohio and Oregon. Beverly pens the award-winning column "Dairy-Free Desserts" in *VegNews* magazine and is the author of *The Complete Idiot's Guide to Vegan Living* and *Eat Your Veggies: Recipes from the Kitchen of the Vegan Chef*. She is also a cooking instructor for the Cancer Project's Food for Life cooking series, which promotes a healthy, plant-based diet for the prevention and survival of cancer (see www.cancerproject.org). Beverly has hosted her own vegan recipe website at VeganChef.com since 1999, which allows her to share her love of vegan food with people all over the world.

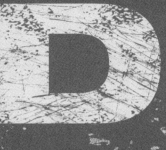

INDEX

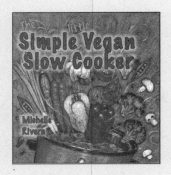